The Proposition

Edinburgh Foundations in Avant-Garde Writing Series List
Series Editors: Georgina Colby and Eric B. White

Published
Her Silver-Tongued Companion: Reading Poems by Harryette Mullen
Harryette Mullen, edited by Georgina Colby

The Proposition: Uncollected Early Poems 1963–1983
Lyn Hejinian

The Proposition
Uncollected Early Poems
1963–1983

Lyn Hejinian
Edited by Georgina Colby

EDINBURGH
University Press

Edinburgh University Press is one of the leading university presses in the UK. We publish academic books and journals in our selected subject areas across the humanities and social sciences, combining cutting-edge scholarship with high editorial and production values to produce academic works of lasting importance. For more information visit our website: edinburghuniversitypress.com

© Lyn Hejinian 2024, 2026
© editorial matter and organisation, Georgina Colby 2024, 2026
© the chapters their several authors 2024, 2026

Published with the support of the University of Edinburgh Scholarly Publishing Initiatives Fund.

First published in hardback by Edinburgh University Press 2024

Edinburgh University Press Ltd
13 Infirmary Street
Edinburgh EH1 1LT

Typeset in 11/13pt Adobe Sabon by
Cheshire Typesetting Ltd, Cuddington, Cheshire, and
printed and bound by CPI Group (UK) Ltd, Croydon, CR0 4YY

A CIP record for this book is available from the British Library

ISBN 978 1 3995 2662 3 (hardback)
ISBN 978 1 3995 5776 4 (paperback)
ISBN 978 1 3995 2664 7 (webready PDF)
ISBN 978 1 3995 2665 4 (epub)

The right of Lyn Hejinian to be identified as the author of this work has been asserted in accordance with the Copyright, Designs and Patents Act 1988, and the Copyright and Related Rights Regulations 2003 (SI No. 2498).

The right of Georgina Colby to be identified as the editor of this work has been asserted in accordance with the Copyright, Designs and Patents Act 1988, and the Copyright and Related Rights Regulations 2003 (SI No. 2498).

Contents

Preface to *The Proposition* viii
Lyn Hejinian

1963–1965	1
The Grreat Adventure (1969–1970)	17
A Month Without Days (1975)	29
The Inclusions (1974–1975)	41
Chronic Texts (1977)	67
1977–1979	81
1979–1981	121
1981–1982	143
1983	173

Critical Essays

The Proposition as Preamble: Lyn Hejinian's Conative Realism 187
Charles Altieri

Early Hejinian 204
Lytle Shaw

Lyn Hejinian's Faustienne Beings-With 215
Emily Critchley

Crossing Improvised Boundaries: Personhood, Poetry, Estrangement 231
Jacob Edmond

The Proposition

Lyn Hejinian's "Allegorical Activism" 254
Jessica Fisher

Chronology of Works 263
Contributors 296
Bibliography 298

With thanks to Paull, Anna, and Larry
who heard it all and stayed

Preface

Lyn Hejinian

The poems collected in this book were written between the summer of 1963 and the summer of 1983, a twenty-year period that began with my graduation from college and ended just before my first trip to the then USSR. Some were published in literary magazines during that period and slightly later (the latest publication was in 1985), many were not, and none have been included in any of my previous books. This last is the case not because I rejected them, but either because I knew virtually nothing about small presses hospitable to new poetry by young poets and therefore didn't know where to submit them (which was the case until around 1975) or because I was beginning to move toward a project-orientated writing practice rather than one focused on individual poems.

The opportunity to look back at and forward from these early poems is one I am grateful for—and I thank Edinburgh University Press and, especially, Georgina Colby, one of the founding editors of the Edinburgh Foundations in Avant-Garde Writing series, for giving me that opportunity. I've organized the poems more or less chronologically—or as chronologically as I could manage. In most cases the typescripts or carbon copies or, in a few cases, the photocopies I was working from are undated, but I had noted on many of them where and when they first appeared in literary magazines; that information, where it exists, has helped me establish a rough chronology. But a number of the poems were either never published or, as is almost certainly the case in some instances, I failed to note the publication information on my copies of them. Even without that information, however, it was clear that clusters of poems were related to each other. In the end, though I'm sure I made some erroneous conclusions as to the order in which they were written, the chronological organization is, in my view, adequately accurate, if not absolutely perfect.

The question before me, as I write this preface, is one that the series title begs: what are we talking about when we evoke the term avant-garde and how are the poems collected here related to it? Initially, in naming this book *The Proposition*, I wanted to suggest that the poems in it can be read as a preamble to, or a rehearsal for, the works of my own that followed from them—the book-length projects that, arguably, were informed by the concerns, both technical and thematic, emerging in them and in the avant-garde unfolding around me. And this rationale still seems valid. But subsequently it has seemed to me, too, that those concerns and the political and aesthetic valences that inform them, might throw some light on what it means to identify or describe certain literary works of the late twentieth (and now early twenty-first) century as avant-garde.

My goal here, however, is not to propose, defend, or advance an argument that the poems in this particular volume represent or exemplify avant-garde writing of the late twentieth century in the United States. Quite apart from the hubris such an undertaking would involve, the fact is that the work of any avant-garde is always collectively created, and no single work is ever comprehensively exemplary of it. From the start then, it includes and depends on sociality and hence on things that exceed individual subjectivities, even though those subjectivities may contribute to or impinge on whatever gets produced. Whether we call this polysubjectivity or dispersed subjectivity or simply social subjectivity matters less than that it belongs to a community and is generated by that community's members.

I'll begin then by positing sociality as a feature of the avant-garde as I know it; sociality is intrinsic to its make-up, shaping and sustaining its creative dynamics and explicitly informing its aspirations. The avant-garde is invariably utopian. To some extent, its utopianism is aspirational and thus oriented toward a future, though what the beautiful topography of that desired future might look like may vary from writer to writer or moment to moment, or it may yet remain unimagined, invisible beyond the horizon, like an unknown future lover or (more likely) a ghost. But the utopia may have a present existence too, not in the form of a new succeeding system but as an ongoing collective creative struggle, activism undertaken in conversation (and sometimes debate) and in the sharing of new works. This is the utopia of the exciting social present, the moment of achievement, fleeting and perhaps for that very reason exhilarating. It is akin to, but not identical with, what Ernst Bloch in *The Principle of Hope* calls concrete utopia. It is utopia as a (necessarily brief and necessarily shared) realized moment.

Prominent theories of the avant-garde have argued that one of its foundational premises is that the present, or something in the present, needs to be overthrown. In this account of the avant-garde, it is said to be out looking for alternatives to the status quo or inventing them or both. I think this argument is often right, but one has to pay attention to what it is that is thought to deserve destruction or, at least, replacement. It may be cultural institutions (one thinks here of Marinetti's call for the destruction of museums), it may be political regimes, it may be reigning social mores, it may be fusty ideas about art and boring representations of them. Or it may be ideologies more broadly, codified narratives underwriting and defending politics, principles, and activities that their opponents judge unjust, unfair, illegal, exploitative, rapacious, and/or simply stupid. In my own involvements with an avant-garde, largely in the context of what has come to be called Language Writing, the matters immediately demanding analysis and critique were systems and structures of language itself, writing's own and only medium. Its power—or array of powers—is not all negative. Inevitably, linguistic systems and structures have ideologies embedded in them, and these are almost always instruments of hegemonic power. But at the same time, language's positive creative and heuristic possibilities are all but infinite, and its ability to excite the imagining faculties (including those that concoct fantasies) and stimulate poesis (the making of neologisms, creative phrases, small and large narratives, as well as descriptions and definitions) is endless in its own ways and seemingly endlessly underway. Language artfully deployed can discover phenomena, develop linkages, and both intensify and expand experience and the realms of the experiential. But of course it can also install ideologies—attitudes, opinions, beliefs, and their attendant practices—and it does so relentlessly and with dictatorial force. It can affect perceptions and establish wide-scale world views that those who hold them don't (and usually can't) question. At the very least, language orients its speakers to whatever world it can articulate. The task for avant-garde writing is to prevent the foreclosure of all others.

It has been argued that avant-garde (experimental) language experiments (in Language writing but in other avant-garde movements as well) aspire to overthrow the tyranny of standard (standardizing) linguistic usages, or, at least, to expose the ways they constrain and control socio-political culture. And this is certainly part of the story. It is right, too, to say that both social (imposed) and psychological (interiorized) identities are constructed, as are morals and mores. So also are rights, interests, borders, laws. Every sentence of every deed, contract, lease, legal agreement, decree, etc., is part of the yellow brick road that leads to and from the throne of the wizard of Oz. Every sentence, often even every word of a sentence, contributes to the ongoing generation of nations, cultures, societies, communities.

This is not as blanket a statement as it might seem, though it refers to one that makes even greater claims. This is what's known as the Sapir-Whorf hypothesis, although nowhere did either linguist (Edward Sapir or Benjamin Lee Whorf) articulate it. I first encountered an uncritically posited version of the hypothesis in a year-long course in linguistic anthropology my first year of college and enthusiastically embraced its implications, both as a critic of English (and especially American English) and as a poet.[1] Roughly, it proposes that

The Proposition

every language carries within it a world view, generally (and to a vast extent unconsciously) held by all the native speakers of that language. One version of the hypothesis, no longer supported by contemporary linguists, holds that every language determines and limits the cognitive consciousness of its speakers. The other states only that language influences perspectival consciousness and our understanding of how the world is structured.

There are various ways to restate (propose) the hypothesis: syntax creates semantics; the world is what we get from language; how you say the world is how you see it. Language may be descriptive, predictive, determinative, prescriptive, restrictive. But it is never fixed, immutable. I can easily (and blandly) say, "Today the ocean is wild," but I can just as easily say, "Today the wild is ocean." And I have.

The Sapir-Whorf hypothesis, then, presents only half the story, and the largely unhappy half at that. It speaks to some important political concerns informing avant-garde linguistic and literary practices, but aesthetic concerns are of at least equal importance in them. Such, at least, has been my experience. Despite its ideological baggage, language can be astutely responsive to the world for which it is always contriving to find names and descriptions, and also alternatives and thus new perspectives (new "takes," new views), intricately alert to appearances of both existent phenomena and will o' the wisps (think of Coleridge's "Frost at Midnight"), and capable of generating illuminating heuristics and achieving astonishing feats of revelatory logic that outsmart the machinations of ideology. Language (*pace* the authors of the *Star Trek* tv series) is able "to boldly go where no one has gone before." And while on its way, it remains receptive to experiences that, so to speak, come to it, responding to incoming intellectual and sensuous information. It makes sense and sensation, but it also receives them, and in both of these complementary processes it contributes materially as well as philosophically to the overlapping realms of meaning and meaningfulness.

The dialectical dynamics that characterize the relationship between the ideology-sustaining and the aesthetic-generating

Preface

capacities of language are premised on a perpetual imbalance between ideology and its opposite, which can't be non-ideology (that's only ideology identified by its lack) but something else, perhaps something purely animal: aesthetic life? raw life? risky life? I posit this not as a revelation; it's just a thought. Though it may be accurate to say that writing poetry can be a way to search out the opposite of ideology, this probably turns out to mean it is just an exercise in opposition: perpetual opposition, perhaps, always in new forms.

Query the narrative; query the grammar; liberate language to construct unimagined conceptual and aesthetic figures. Such a program, whether one calls it tinkering with the machine, throwing wrenches into its works, or writing with a hammer (to appropriate Nietzsche's description of his philosophizing), bears its own ideology, of course. Even Nietzsche's call for a perpetual revaluation of all values ("philosophy of the future") and Leslie Scalapino's call for "continual conceptual rebellion" assume certain foundational givens and advocate for certain kinds of outcome, however short-lived those may be. But in this whole project, Modernism's "make it new" becomes the present's demand for more than novelty. Critique is asked to go wild; language is invited to play. Ideally, the result is adventure: flowing and fluctuating thought, currents of contingency, chance, confusion as well as confluence, risks, lies, errors, meanders. And experience at a fully literal level. Stone storage sequences played by fated actors—take it literally!

This may all seem somewhat abstract, but in fact poems are written from within lived lives. Such is certainly the case for the poems collected here. And, though direct references or discernable details from the lived life that was my own when I was writing them are rare, that life is more than background to the poems. In their peculiar ways, the poems embrace it. And both polysubjectivity and the experience of present moment utopias characteristic of commitment to sociality are, I hope, embedded in those collected here.

The Proposition is organized into nine sections. The first comprises a set of five poems that were written between the

The Proposition

summer of 1963 and late 1965, a period that began when, married and newly graduated from college, I moved from Cambridge (Massachusetts) to an apartment a few blocks away from Harvard Medical School. My then husband began medical school in 1963 and our first child was born in 1964. Dissatisfied with the education I'd received—or, rather, aware of how little I knew of English and American literature despite having majored in English—I was reading both historically (using George Saintsbury's *History of English Literature* as my guide to the literary history of England) and within what I thought of as "my world"—Modernist and contemporary works: Joyce, Proust, Lawrence Ferlinghetti, Kenneth Patchen, Virginia Woolf, Faulkner, Gertrude Stein. I thought of myself as a Beatnik, but I didn't wander far from the canon, or at least those parts of it that, though aesthetically radical, were accepted as "important." I won't argue with that last judgment: they were and are important. But, apart from English translations of Japanese and Chinese poetry and the Edward Fitzgerald translation of *The Rubáiyát of Omar Khayyam* (!), I had little to no contact with non-European literature. I was also reading travel literature, works written in the seventeenth, eighteenth, and nineteenth centuries. My then husband and I with our eight-month-old child spent much of the summer of 1965 in and around Lausanne, Switzerland, where my father had a two-year academic position; I read books about alpine hiking and we did some modest hiking of our own.

The five poems of the second section of *The Proposition* are all from what was intended to be a book published in a comic book format. And, in fact, such publication happened—sort of. Under the title *The Grreat Adventure* and at my own expense, around 100 copies were printed by Don Donahue (the publisher of Zap Comix, R. Crumb's first comic books) in 1972. The book had no distribution and I ended up owning most of the copies myself until they were destroyed in 1973, the victims of heavy rain, lack of storage space, and my own carelessness. My first marriage had ended, and I'd moved with my two children (the second was born in

1966) and the musician Larry Ochs to an undeveloped piece of land in inland Mendocino County; we were building a cabin and, with no place to put the cartons, I left them under an oak tree. *The Grreat Adventure* was very much a product of 1969–1970: a miscellany of political anecdotes interwoven with poems about sex, love, drugs, and outer space and bedecked with psychedelic drawings, rubber stamped images, and press type transfers (mostly letters). A section of the comic is a description and record of a project I did in 1969 with the San Francisco-based visual artist Doug Hall (who happens to be my brother).

The third and fourth sections of *The Proposition* both date from 1974–6. The first is a single poem ("A Month Without Days") and the second includes twenty-one poems from a never published (and never submitted) manuscript titled *The Inclusions*. At the time, inland Mendocino County was home to a number of "back-to-the-land hippies," people living to some degree off-the-grid (or off some grid) and trying to forge social and personal alternatives to the regimens and values of "mainstream America," in which, though we didn't yet have the term for it, the neoliberal socio-economic order, along with a concomitant form of capitalism, was becoming dominant. The kinds of news to which William Carlos Williams so famously referred when he wrote (in "Asphodel, That Greeny Flower") "it is difficult / to get the news from poems / yet men die miserably every day / for lack / of what is found there" was not readily available in the area—there were no bookstores, no museums, no theaters, and the nearest public library was tiny and had almost no poetry on its shelves. We made the three-hour drive to San Francisco once a month, and it was at City Lights Books that I found small press publications and books from presses like Black Sparrow, Burning Deck, New Directions, and, of course, City Lights. I took a part time job at the Willits Print Shop and founded Tuumba Press, whose format was largely inspired by the chapbooks that Black Sparrow was putting out, mostly to publicize the books it was publishing, and chapbooks from Burning Deck Press. I started corresponding with Susan Howe, Ron

The Proposition

Silliman, Maureen Owen, Rosmarie Waldrop and continued corresponding with Ken Irby, whom I'd known since 1961. It's tempting to say that *The Inclusions*, the title I gave the 1974–5 poems, was meant to give a nod to the expansion of the contexts I was writing in, and that may be the case. There definitely seemed to be a lot of space in which to include things, a benefit of living at the top of a ridge surrounded by ranchland and high chaparral.

In July 1977, we moved to Berkeley and exchanged ridge-top benefits for those of the San Francisco Bay Area's new experimental literary and improvised music scenes.[2] The problematics of time—simultaneity, nonlinearity (and devices like collage and, especially, montage), chronicity and anachronism, memory and forgetting, historiography and narrative, repetition, and, for a while and above all, present time—continued to preoccupy me. "Chronic Texts" was written for presentation in the Talks series that Bob Perelman curated in the San Francisco loft space that he shared with the painter Francie Shaw (his wife). It's an account of returns—reiterations as they register differences in the endlessly changing and proliferative contexts in which they recur. And each of the poems in the sixth (1977–9) section of *The Proposition* has an indexical character, the present as a moment of habitation, created not by a subject (here presumably the poet) but by another, the presence (and hence presentness) of someone or something else.

Meanwhile, in my immersion in the developing Language writing scene, questions of literary form and linguistic systems were becoming increasingly significant. Literary acknowledgment of the lived present moment is often indicated by the grammatical present tense or by indexical phrases (phrases pointing to presences by naming them), but that present tense was in no way a simple present, grammatical or otherwise. And the otherness of subjectivity (the presence acknowledging the present) was polyphonic, rather than singular or even a set or sequence of alternative psychosocial positions. In 1978, after many weeks of rehearsal, Steve Benson, Carla Harryman, Barrett Watten, Kit Robinson,

Preface

Bob Perelman and I did several public performances of Louis Zukofsky's "'A'-24," scored for voices and piano, and that same group of people plus several more began meeting once a week to read and discuss the entirety of Zukofsky's "A." Barrett already had a long-standing interest in the Modernist epic, and partially under that influence I took the epic seriously, not as a genre or form but as a method, the germ of a poetics. It opened a way out of constrictive lyric modes, too often bound to local subjectivity, and into large-scale and largely social commitments and their ensuing projects.

Epic, then, as a medium for the making of social culture and very much connected to Language writing, provided me with models for poetry. Length per se was of negligible interest; composite form, and indeed form-making itself (constructivism), were major concerns. I was sympathetic to the call to "include everything" (which was articulated most often by women poets at the time), but almost by definition anything that has form gains its contours by admitting limits, and my attention was often focused on negotiating competing desires: to admit or even seek out the contingent, to follow streams of association, and/or to acknowledge the perpetual breakdown of any autonomy that any present moment or presence could pretend to. Each of these seemed equally accurate to my experience of being in the world, but they were all but mutually exclusive, not only as different possibilities but as guiding principles for individual works.

In retrospect I can speculate that a guiding principle of my own work has been the pursuit of inquiry and exploration, supported either by uncertainty and skepticism or by curiosity and excessive (or restless) enthusiasm. The last three sections of *The Proposition* present work in different modes—modal adventures, so to speak. Some, no doubt, respond to ideas I developed (or appropriated) from work I was hearing at poetry readings and in conversations before and after them and to the explicit turn to poetics, as represented in the thirteen issues of *L=A=N=G=U=A=G=E* magazine (co-edited by Bruce Andrews and Charles Bernstein in New York) that appeared between 1978 and 1981 and in the ten issues of

The Proposition

Poetics Journal (co-edited by Barrett Watten and me in the San Francisco Bay Area) that appeared between 1982 and 1998.[3] Pieces published in these two complementary though very different journals chart the communal development of a social as well as aesthetic praxis, one which foregrounded the interdependence of poetry and poetics, not as the site of individual creativity or expression but as a multifaceted engagement in the elaboration of a consciously social (and sometimes transhistorical and transcultural) project.

What, then, did (or does) *The Proposition* propose? Looking at the works from a distance, one could claim that they argue for linguistic processes that dismantle (or, in the earliest work, reconfigure) received structures of perception and interpretation and posit others that excite new perceptions and new interpretations. This is not to say that they succeed at this, only that it is what they aspired to. A quick (and inevitably incomplete) list of the aesthetic and/or social structures the poems in *The Proposition* were exploring include narrative (and its falsities as well as its inventive and interpretative capacities); linguistic syntax (and its constructive, intensifying, and contextualizing powers as well as its conditioning force); subjectivity (in its disarray, its ability to play, pretend, or even metamorphose, and in its disappearance from the scene altogether); and linguistic materiality (bearing the recombinatory potential of letters, morphemes, and phonemes). There are others, but, even incomplete as it is, this list should suggest that there were creatively positive as well as politically urgent reasons (motivations) driving the kinds of experimentation evident in poems like those collected here.

It seems worth giving some thought for a moment to the status of some of the more "difficult" (intransigent or opaque) poems or passages within poems—those in this volume or those by some of the other poets whose work is identified with Language writing. Ray DiPalma once characterized his own poems as "lapidary," but, insofar as that might suggest they are impermeable, concise, or adamantine, that characterization, I believe, does a disservice to the poems. The point

Preface

is for so-called difficult poems to contain enough negativity that they can depetrify or decommodify themselves. Here I would argue against Adorno's insistence on the autonomy of the work of art. Writers—and avant-garde writers of my historical period and scene in particular—repeatedly call the aesthetic (in its narrower sense, as synonymous with art rather than as a term for sense experiences more generally) into question. Their writings, in attempting to counter the obsolescence of received forms, expose themselves to the world in which those forms are said to have value and where writers can discover or invent alternative new forms and new conceptual possibilities. In paradoxical ways, the poems become narrative precisely by not being so. That is, the writings reformulate context. And in doing so, they seek their story at least in part by countering current stories.

It is here, finally, that propositionality comes into play, functioning sometimes as a prod, sometimes for the sake of speculation and invention, and sometimes heuristically. In preparing this volume for publication, I couldn't help but notice the frequency with which declarative sentences (or sentences grammatically constructed so that they have the semantic force of declaration) occur. It was not my intention to make declarations per se, though the proclivity of the so-called simple sentence in American English for making truth claims is remarkable (and probably for the most part regrettable), and I admit to having often been fascinated by it. But my own interest in the rhetoric of claims and propositions lies in the character of the fantasy states or hypothetical situations they have the power to animate, as if a statement could flick a switch and throw a spotlight simultaneously on an invented world, on the inventing imagination, and on the "magic" language that brings things to pass. In this sense, propositions may serve as points of departure, even when they are disguised as points of arrival. In writing them, I have experienced them as epistemological forays—tests and experiments.

But what did I want to know? Or, rather, to know about? Aesthesis itself, perhaps: experience. Experiencing as an expansive existential commitment: conscious existing as a

The Proposition

made and making proposition. Very much has changed since the two decades during which the works collected here were written; the world as we have it now provides very different contexts, different possibilities, and different limits for the making of consciousness. The poetry and poetry movements that I was encountering between 1963 and 1983 were all integral to Modernism (early and late) and to North American participation in its unfolding (as late Modernism and then Postmodernism). The field was immense and new information was constantly becoming available, both in new anthologies and in just published translations of new (and a few early) philosophical and theoretical texts coming out of Europe, the UK, and the USSR. These included feminist and post-colonial theory and predecessors to queer theory.[4] But many of these latter appeared after 1983; prior to that much of the information was coming out of Anglo-European socio-political and cultural contexts. And that was a limit condition.

Given this, and viewed now in retrospect but also from both a present time and a prospective vantage point, one can say that the Language project was not—and is not—perfect. But, in my view, imperfection is one of its potential strengths: it remains unfinished, incomplete, underway, and—as the world around it changes—it remains expansive, a dynamic force in what Barrett Watten and I, in the subtitle to *A Guide to Poetics Journal*, referred to as the "expanded field" (*A Guide to Poetics Journal: Writing in the Expanded Field 1982–1998*); as I remember it, the term was Barrett's, and I think that he would agree when I say that its expansion continues today. I would add, too, that the Language project was never as limited nor as "imperfect" as its critics have claimed, but arguing (and hopefully demonstrating) that belongs in a different document from this one. For now, I will let the predicate "imperfect" stand, not because it's particularly apt—it definitely isn't—but because it names a catalyst for change (expansion) and not just the stasis of failure.

For the imperfections of an artistic movement to succeed as a motivating rather than terminal condition, it must be accompanied by social as well as individual sources of energy and something closely resembling (though not, I think, identical to) principled authority—what I would term shared commitment. Those sources of energy may include friendship or revolutionary camaraderie or political anger (and/or grief) or any number of other things. And expenditures of energy (or even the willingness to contribute energy) are rarely if ever equally divided among all the members of a group. But it is equally true that such conditions as psychosocial dispiritedness, exhaustion, a preference for social or individual ease rather than fervor or struggle, and so forth need not overcome an aesthetic movement tout court.

Some individuals may age (or age themselves) out of a group's aesthetic activism and capacity for protestation as well as for radical creativity, but, at least with respect to the Language project, it is a misperception to consider its power (or that of its practitioners) as, now fifty years on, ebbing away or to imagine that its contributions to the history and to the present time reality of poetry and poetics are turning out to be less significant or less beneficial (or, as some have claimed, more harmful) than they seemed one to five decades ago.

That said, the political, economic, climatological, social (and, especially, the demographic), and even biological contexts that constitute the contemporary "world" in which poetry and poetics (and cultural practices more widely) exist are very different now from what they were in the early days of Language writing. The hegemony of white cultural production over all others in the US is an unhappy condition that Cedric Robinson explores amply in his classic 1983 *Black Marxism: The Making of the Black Radical Tradition*, though the notion itself does not originate with Robinson.[5]

Much of the cultural production of the last quarter of the twentieth and first quarter of the twenty-first centuries in the US means differently than it did from the 1960s to the Reagan presidency, since the making of its meaning is in the hands of new readers dealing with new challenges, new realities, and—at last!—new sites and sources of cultural power. These new readers, like those who create the new texts and

The Proposition

performances they care about, are no longer primarily (if at all) heirs to a Euro/Anglocentric Modernism but to other traditions and visions. The white supremacist foundations of the US continue to assert power and control over many institutions and ideological systems, but people of color, along with women and people from LGBTQ+ communities are prominently and influentially initiating and participating in much of the creative culture of today, which includes film, dance, visual art, performance, music (which, of course, has never lacked a Black presence, though too often presented to white audiences in consumable form), and writing, but also opinion, at least in the so-called "Liberal media." The "avant-garde" of today is a site of intergenerational and intersectional sociality, one that can feel now as if it is happening "naturally" or "organically," though in fact it is a result of decades of work by people of color as well as by radical (and not always so radical) white activists. It is also one in which Language writing, seen as a white-dominated movement, is sometimes dismissed or even attacked. "To encounter the history of avant-garde poetry is to encounter a racist tradition," as Cathy Park Hong remarks in her essay "Delusions of Whiteness in the Avant-Garde."[6]

This is a remark to which Aldon Lynn Nielsen and many others, myself included, might object, not as a judgment but as a statement of fact. Nielsen acknowledges (in *Black Chant: Languages of African-American Postmodernism*) that "critics of white poetry [...] seldom look at black writers while compiling their genealogies of aesthetic evolution," but, as Nielsen convincingly demonstrates, their work is not only present, it is an essential participant in the collective formation and evolution of experimental poetry in the US.[7] Nielsen's emphasis in *Black Chant* is on the interconnections between linguistic experimentation in literature, on the one hand, and traditions of Black vernacular language and improvisatory practices on the other. Zora Neale Hurston, in her 1934 essay "The Characteristics of Negro Expression," offers a slightly alternative focus, on what she terms "drama" and "action words," many instances of which involve what

Henry Louis Gates Jr. characterizes as "signifyin'," a linguistic practice that draws explicitly on Black improvisational music and that Gates describes as a "complex act of language [that] Signifies upon both formal language use and its conventions, conventions established, at least officially, by middle-class white people."⁸ He amplifies his discussion of the critical distinction between Signifyin(g) and signification with multiple examples of the former, but he is aware of European contexts in which such discussions came to the fore (in, for example, the work of the Swiss linguist Ferdinand de Saussure, the Russian philosopher Mikhail Bakhtin, and the French psychoanalyst Jacques Lacan). As he puts it "We bear witness here to a protracted argument over the nature of the sign itself, with the black vernacular discourse proffering its critique of the sign as the difference that blackness makes within the larger political culture and its historical unconscious."⁹ This "difference that blackness makes" seems not to have registered in the European context.

Nor does it seem to have done so in that of "The Politics of the Referent," the forum that appeared in the summer 1977 issue of the Canadian journal *Open Letter*. Edited by Steve McCaffery (whose long first essay, "The Death of the Subject: The Implications of Counter-Communication in Recent Language-Centered Writing," is one of the forum's best), its other contributors were Bruce Andrews, Ray DiPalma, Ron Silliman, and Charles Bernstein, a group (noticeably all male and white) of avant-garde writers whose ideas drew heavily on Marx and on new theoretical writing by emerging major European thinkers that was just appearing in English translation. The primary and predominant concern, especially for Silliman, McCaffery, and Andrews, was with class struggle as the root cause not only of socio-political and economic injustice but of their structural manifestations throughout any given culture. Racialization and racism were seen as the products of classism, or, since this is the form that it took (and takes), of white supremacist ideology and practices. Misogyny, even in its minor "everyday" forms, may have been deemed similar, but it most often seemed to belong to another realm altogether. "Female" was certainly not the name of an identifiable social class.

Of what then is it the name?

Answering that question at length would take this "Preface" far from its intended purpose and from the context for which it is written. But the question does return us to the question of signifiers. Black American vernacular culture is hardly the place to look for anti-misogyny and gender fluidity or gender equity, but its tendency to turn away from abstractions in order to attend to actual present time linguistic transactions and practices continues and extends the work that Signifyin(g) exemplifies and that Language writing from its inception, as a critique of hegemonic power structures and the language that underwrites and purveys them, has undertaken.

As Henry Louis Gates Jr. observes, "Signifyin(g) turns on the play and chain of signifiers, and not on some supposedly transcendent signified."[10] It is this "transcendental signified," the hegemonic pre-established gang of referents embedded in a system that exercises its tyrannical hold on language and turns words, phrases, and even grammar into fetishized commodities, that, early in the development of Language writing, the *Open Letter* forum exposed. As McCaffery put it in his brief prefatory comments, "[W]hat Marx exposed as the fetishism of commodity is the same mode of mystification that is enacted in the fetishism of the referent, both being instruments for the displacement of human relations into an iconography of commodity."[11] And (McCaffery again), "The demand is for praxis not consumption".[12]

It is a praxis that the works of *The Proposition* propose: an opening of linguistic possibility not for the sake of a subject (either as a unitary personal self or as an external topic or theme). And one prominent methodological element in play is obscurity—"spontaneous and authentic obscurity, a characteristic phenomenon of the most genuinely modern art," as the Italian scholar of comparative literature Renato Poggioli said in *The Theory of the Avant-Garde*.[13] Or, as Bruce Andrews puts it, "'Unreadability'—that which requires new readers, and teaches new readings."[14]

Preface

According to what Poggioli terms the "doctrines" of an avant-garde determined to overthrow the musty, rotten, petrified structures of a cultural status quo, "the linguistic obscurity of contemporary poetry should exercise a function at once cathartic and therapeutic in respect to the degeneration afflicting common language through convention and habits. The quasi-private idiom of our lyric poetry would then have a social end, would serve as a corrective to the linguistic corruption characteristic of any mass culture [. . .] Poetic obscurity would then aim at creating a treasure trove of new meanings within the poverty of common language, a game of multiple, diverse, and opposing meanings."[15]

Ron Silliman ends his contribution to the *Open Letter* forum with the lovely, though perhaps melodramatic, valediction "Permanent Revolution." Just before that he writes, "Language-centered writing can take many forms. It is first of all activity that is conscious of itself [. . .] It is the first step (and only that) of the return of the poem to the people. It is a politicized poem and not a 'political poem' (which is a counter-tendency occurring within the commodity fetish). It tells you that these words are empty until you fill them with your presence, reading them, being them. Together, you and these words could do anything."[16]

Demographic variousness and intersectional sociality (and therefore an expanded array of political, cultural, and aesthetic practices and visions) are now a vital part of the US avant-garde poetry scene(s). As a result, new emphases and new modes of creative consciousness and participatory poetics have emerged, and more are to come. It behooves us all to be fearless and attentive to these and to participate as readers even as we attempt to do work worthy of reciprocal attention. And it behooves us, as always, to be skeptical (it is with our skepticism that we maintain inner freedom) but also to be surprised, confused, concerned, and delighted.

Just as it did forty-five years ago, Language writing today advocates for consciousness (which should not be confused with conventional logic or reason), political as well as aesthetical motivations, resistance to (or, dare I say, rebellion against) hegemonic ideologies and their instantiation in social and economic and political systems, and perpetual engagement in critique and reevaluation of values, precepts, and practices, including (especially?) its own. Both as a method and as a practice, Language writing maintains what, in an early (1983) essay of mine, I termed "the rejection of closure."[17]

Can one apply this last also to the future? Much—most—of what we (or I) imagine in and as the future gives us a grim prospect of closure, the end result of cannibalistic exploitation, devastation, ruin. There will be a future, certainly—some kind of future—but prospects for planetary well-being there seem entirely bleak. But there is one exception to this. The one area of human (and I think not exclusively human) activity whose future existence may be a site and source of wonder and creative excitement is that of art. Early in my "Introduction" to *The Language of Inquiry*, I wrote, "Language is nothing but meanings, and meanings are nothing but a flow of contexts."[18] If the contexts are bleak or in ruin, then the meanings will be too. But avant-garde writing not only has its own contexts; it also creates its own contexts, and it is possible to describe those not principally in terms of the external realities of the world but, rather, as things that writers and readers do with words within them. It is not wrong to continue to call Language writing (and other, related avant-garde movements) utopian—dedicated to a good future, albeit one that doesn't exist (yet). Art and its makers must make sure that today—today the wild is ocean.

Notes

1. See, for example, "Barbarism," in Lyn Hejinian, *The Language of Inquiry* (Berkeley: University of California Press, 2000), 318–54.
2. For a discussion of experimental improvisational music in the Bay Area and its influence on Language writing, see

Preface

Lyn Hejinian, "Taking to the Music," in *The Grand Piano: An Experiment in Collective Autobiography 1975–1980*, co-authored by Rae Armantrout, Steve Benson, Carla Harryman, Lyn Hejinian, Tom Mandel, Ted Pearson, Bob Perelman, Kit Robinson, Ron Silliman, and Barrett Watten (ten parts; Detroit: Mode A, 2006–10), part 7 (pp. 50–74).

3. Many of the poetry readings took place at a coffee house in San Francisco called The Grand Piano. For a composite memoir of the literary scene around those and related readings in the Bay Area at the time, see *Grand Piano*. The full run of *L=A=N=G=U=A=G=E* can be found at http://eclipsearchive.org/projects/LANGUAGE/language.html. A selection of essays and works from *Poetics* journal can be found in Lyn Hejinian and Barrett Watten, *A Guide to Poetics Journal: Writing in the Expanded Field, 1982–98* (University Presses of New England/Wesleyan University Press, 2013) and almost all the essays and works from the journal (lacking all but two short pieces) are available in Lyn Hejinian and Barrett Watten, eds., *Poetics Journal Digital Archive* (ebook; Wesleyan University Press, 2015).

4. See the appendix to the co-authored (Rae Armantrout, Steve Benson, Carla Harryman, Lyn Hejinian, Tom Mandel, Ted Pearson, Bob Perelman, Kit Robinson, Ron Silliman, and Barrett Watten) *Grand Piano*, part 7 for a chronological (and inevitably incomplete) list of books published between 1975 and 1980 and significant for the volume's authors; Armantrout et al., *Grand Piano*, part 7 (Detroit: Mode A, 2008).

5. See Cedric Robinson, *Black Marxism: The Making of the Black Radical Tradition* (Chapel Hill: The University of North Carolina Press, 1983), especially chapter I: "Racial Capitalism: The Nonobjective Character of Capitalist Development" and chapter V, pp. 109–20.

6. Cited without source in Molly McArdle, "'I Arrived at the Revolution Via Poetry': An Interview with the Mongrel Coalition Against Gringpo," *Brooklyn Magazine*, July 15, 2015, online at https://www.bkmag.com/2015/07/22/i-arrived-at-the-revolution-via-poetry-an-interview-with-the-mongrel-coalition-against-gringpo/ (accessed September 8, 2022).

7. Aldon Lynn Nielsen, *Black Chant: Languages of African-American Postmodernism* (Cambridge: Cambridge University Press, 1997), 13.

8. Henry Louis Gates Jr., *The Signifying Monkey: A Theory of African American Literature* (Oxford: Oxford University Press, 1989), 47.
9. Gates, *The Signifying Monkey*, 45.
10. Gates, *The Signifying Monkey*, 52.
11. McCaffery, *Open Letter*, 60.
12. McCaffery, *Open Letter*, 71
13. Renato Poggioli, *The Theory of the Avant-Garde*, trans. Gerald Fitzgerald (Cambridge, MA: The Belknap Press of Harvard University Press, 1968), 152.
14. Bruce Andrews, "Text and Context," in Frank Davey, ed., *Open Letter*, Third Series, no. 7 (summer 1977) (Toronto, Canada), 78.
15. Poggioli, *The Theory of the Avante-Garde*, 37–8.
16. Ron Silliman, "from aRb," in in Frank Davey, ed., *Open Letter*, Third Series, no. 7 (summer 1977) (Toronto, Canada).
17. Hejinian, *The Language of Inquiry*, 40–58.
18. Hejinian, *The Language of Inquiry*, 1.

1963–1965

Adam of the Animals

    a. HE COULD CHARM

And he can spell.
Because of this he is the mastermock,
Mac, important one,
let's say of solar equinity.
Everyday at the same time the horses
hit the sea. It is my specious power
and a very special pleasure, he says.
He says, 'Lion
and lamb' and is glad
in the jungle and on the farm.

    b. WHAT THEY CALL YOU IS HOW THEY SEE YOU

It's who you are, Invisible; it's who you say
you are. The image of your law is Mac, down
a reality to earth, and that
makes Grandpa happy. Mutually magical
and mysteriously are he
and his becoming name.
It are his mighty shirts.
It are his minute shirts. Significantly
it is his sheet.
And it was Grandpa's shawl.
                        O Mac

The Proposition

is my Mac, the anagogue
and summing up; and it must be kept
from the shaman. I have thoughts.
I have deep feelings, says Mac.
There are my legs and these my lips.
My hands are clean and fingernails trimmed.
But I am Adam, I am Mac, a reality
like the riddle of the eye that thieves
and leaves what it thieves.
                      O Onymous Mac,
Adam with a name, it makes you blush.

c. THE AUGMENT OF IMAGISTE

Adam when he's imagiste is Mac sweet
mécanique making jewel
and jouet of the world; and all the while
making with the purity of name.
The sun (plain morning upon sea)
is synonymous with nankeen glow
that's growing all about the name of sun
and sea as simple speech
can be. (Fire
and water, imagiste, and the sea whose spray
is ash on tree.) The ivory tusk
of the elephant, leaf, and the word, leaf,
rain on grain, and the rocks
we share there where they are island totems
lengthen, as are shadows to the sun.

d. ADAM MAKES A GAME OF NAME

We are two things but one, the green expression
from a budding thought, rustling
and the utterance of rustle.
This is a panting forest.
And did trees bark, I'd be the green tongue
of a brown dog and with it what he woofed.

e. THE QUALIFICATION OF ADAM, OR MAC

Adam, Nomenclator, 's calling names.
That's his reminder of things. He makes romance
that is reality, enchantment
with the law that lies between ideas
of rock and rock. But
          Mac
the Master, you nice man, some mute beast he named
may have its mystery there
where the rocks we share are island
totem
and you can't do much but sit and stare.

Published in *The Minnesota Review*, vol. VIII, no. 4 (1968)
Alvin Greenberg, editor

Lines that draw the firstborn's birth

Lines that draw the firstborn's birth
shape an altared figure. he is an offering
we'll keep and care for. hushabye.
goolulladbye. for suddenly the gleeman
goes and there's no more a muffin man
in drury lane.
              this is an art for solace,
sweet rhymes drawing years into mountains
borne over by lullumbering bears. now my son
rises in my stead, daring me to bear him.
the ceaseless fathers, and constant mothers,
who once laid promises at my feet, laid them
not, alas, for me. gone with the gleeman
and the baker who marked it with B. does a lord
pipe over his sleep as she lulled as I lullabye
him? slowlyric do we with the gleeman go
and quicklyric wander quickening our own
flesh and fleshback with another's. as our ashes,
ashes, but that too passes,
as did the muffin man down drury lane.

Published in *The Laurel Review*, vol. 1, no. 1 (spring 1966)

The River Nets the Peninsula
A nursery rhyme

the river nets the peninsula. all the rest
are fishes flowing through okeanid fingerweeds
like fertile sand, or silt, with one foot tucked
beneath the other island riding. a dawnple
upon the water.
                a messofish, said Bertha
Hewitt, out like a messofish,
in and out the circle. my breasts they call bellies.
out of the opulent rievery, prolific mornings
out of beds. borne up borne up, and keep the baby
from the river, she calls. the sprite and hungry
call for fresheggs and cream as rich as dreams.
to the familial breaktoast gathered round they come
in a row like scales. the first we made our Mark,
        his words,
and the daughter Donna climbs from the delta.
    whoaup,
her whoart beats. there's so much river, she says,
Sam almost drowned and got his feet wet.
o ho the riparian frogs leap
for water, later the tadpoles leap for shore.
                                 Horace
Hewitt mellifluous drunk
       by the yellow riveroom, shadown, boom roam
       in the floodsblood the crackling creatures
       and painted dragons are teeming, paddy
born in the dillweed
he's the salt
of the earth, his wife, Bertha Hewitt is. with an eye
turned inward and an eye out for riches.

The Proposition

    her children like toads in the mud or primitives
    behind mud masks preserved in the boggy. while
    Horace dreams he says of streaming winebarrelsful
    whereupon each is written
    Come, Horace Hewitt, draw and drink.
        that, he says,
        is the finnest pote potted,
        and the finnest finnest potery.
    (to my son
    who has brought and blessed the wave down broken
    on the shore.)

    down by the murged riverine
    tipdipt into the flow like swans, drinking horses
    drunk, raccoons that wash their food and feet. (the reeds
    they root so peacefully, she muses briefly absorbed.)
    up and forth, back and to,
    the mounding banks and bounding river by, shelving
    sundairy chosen on the shores. between the eyes
          and knows
    of the hills, each cliff and ledge the rocks built
    imaginable: his face, her face, the hindquarters
    of a grazing mare. (eyes and knows, he laughs.)
    further upstream, 'twixt the lips whence the flume flows
    in browken wrinkles, sphinxen old and enigmatic,
    lie the still fat flats
    where the river has been poured out over the landtop,
    a bog of peace not deep enough to drown in.
    down by the riverine
                the suns
    a daycomequickcreek.   ev, he addressed
    the flowing
           in a babeling
    gwa brook's a baby river out
    in August's dream days (Lored, the ponds
    never freeze until they're full, Horace told me).
    augustly there they purposefully play. Mark,
    get out of the water your lips are blue. that's ink,
    he says, I'm a poet. so says your father, she answers,
    now come sit on the plank and plash your feet
    if you must in the pool.

split splat fishelldy sam
standing above the old mill dam
splish splash nowee sallwet
and that, said the fish, is what you get.
from here's where we watch what's coming down,
    she says,
upon the overbearing riverapt plank that touches shore
to shore. thinngs that are. aren't, he says,
in eager assertiveness. just like so can't I,
eye can. riverbirch and milky way.
Vitis vulpina. all there is to be,
and meant it. dreams and good digestion are.
leap frog over the plank, turtle on the log,
pheasant, muskrat, mouse, richly berried bushes
and creature riverbanks (bear more than coins).
censor no details.
sobeit: my panultimate benediction (before the inevitable
    separation)
cancel no images.
        yet the children continue to ask
        do all rivers un to the sea?
the ev is so mild, the current cx past
and xc lappaps. in byb, child.
                tllk tllk
from the liquid rivermouth
deltoothed, the awords of sounding.

sdeeper. the dust smells like honey,
says Donna. you know blueberries when they rot
smell like sweet wet wool.   o ho, says Horace, the dust
drapes deep the dust drapes deep the dust
drapes deep the dust dapes dreep the dohoho
hewn out of wood, she says.
    hoarse. he approaches with drink
    and she shouts atim horse, gid
    or shut. but all is forgiven,
    I make no reproaches.

what can the alpha beta elephant do
with twenty-six laces tying his shoe?
                dance

The Proposition

o river river river thrice o children
of care and carefor fond dotey fond am I.
in this backstep backstep backstep dancegame
(hey, says Mark, look out you'll fall in) I step
into the center and circle around, it
at the heart of a sphere I see
from afar.
   I'm bursted
from being so full, says Donna. I'm now bust,
all of us. ripe in the garden. has Sam enough teeth
for tomatoes? run it off around the tree then,
Mark answers.
   I cannot catch her; I cannot catch myself.
   untagging it forever.
the surface broken, flung up in silver ropes.

(to my son
in his oblivious innocent amoral sleep
and the energies spent in making the circle turn.)

into the night good the day barges, ropeset,
thus the travels of tempustation, withowl hoot
or whistle and pursued by the children who have run
and playn after all day (nonobjective lovers
out of focus); past them and us, peregrinations
of the river, what a work it is.
     then a dream
allnight of day replete, up dawnoonight down
flowing like an augur or goldaurose sign
of the morrow repeated. iconographic bankbeasts,
symbols of plenty, bedded in the horn of Amalthaea,
a revelrous rivery, riot of rifewife, a reverent
   flumenous soul
in meternity. breath be arth fecund
out of riverot. (the river nets the peninsula.)
amen ram-headed.
   tllk tllk.
the owl calls hewitt, hewitt, and the quail.
hee-ew. witt!
   riverman riverman where do you go
   along the riverbed?

up to the mountains or down to the sea
wherever I am led.

riverman riverman where do you go
around the riverbend?
over the rapids and down in the pools
until the waters end.
unbottled up he says.
high and inebright, riches. hoarse
as a parrot but brightbeautifully feathered.
coxcombed like the garden rooster through the goldenrod,
pepperth and saw't. ah ah ah my birth, think how abundant
the earth and how. dower me that, old nanny nursey goat.
eyes mind heart and belly, my oldated. the belly
that belies the obscure love. embreacst.
                            the mares backed
to the dophiont northwind; mounts them.
                                        cx xc tllk o
o she an' us. bodybend, shugged,
and finally in the riverbed cx xc. the ev.
ni, she says.
            dawnight to. downight inexorable.
so they go, so they grow
                        into the heart
of it flooding with opulence
and vulnerability
                  hopelessly silent moths
how to . . . that I accept and submit to o the . . .
sentunder and get bliss them. I gowunderfull.
slips past, riverruns.
let it sleep then, let them.
                            riveruns
sethisunsandowns
scalethemergeverainarrowateriveroverapids
soriverimbibeatheasiness
softhearthoneyellowealthateems
sofecundammedeeplentyieldingreateriches
serpentineaseawardropastheatedayoungirls
sleepetulantheiredimouths
stillazilyethroughoursweetlyawningoes
stagnanthenextouterillslowetrills

The Proposition

sleepereachomewardownightips
sweethebbendeltandrops
swifterivereacheshoresandreamazes.

Come, Horace Hewitt, draw and drink.

Published in *Beloit Poetry Journal* (fall 1968)
Marion Stocking, editor

Ophelia

to have so touched the beauty of oblivion
like death, which she did find too lovely
beneath the lily pads. like bliss, is sleeping
innocence, and does one chasten. she sleeps
suspended and ever, after that soft first
tentative taste of the ambrosial Lethe. who loved
and erred thus loving lost not her grace, so fondly doting.
wherefor the mad are made trebly wise, said the doctor,
once for themselves, once for others, and once
and for all. if that is sleep, the dawn lies
on the other riverbank. a plaintive artful fool.
of this there's no renewal now the rapine flood
besought upholds her. and yet the pale silk
seems still to weight her walking.
                              I would that I were
wooed again, she said, though dapple-dammed
beneath the twilit trees. outreaching hand for hand
in the madwoman's angelic posture of erring
supplication. he said we would be fleet and gold
as the gray sky's parting. and raucous
as riddles. ah, so cruelly does romance progress
and gull itself. get thee, get thee. thyself. while
the doves above the window are cooing. wooed
and dapple-damned beneath the twilit trees.
                              a laugh,
a leap, no more the cadence of her chosen speech.
beside a clown beneath a play of swords
(which in the wedding crossed the bride;
I licked the frosting from the blade and charity
was changed at last, and charged with more

The Proposition

than her soul's keeping). the paper turns to dust
the wind shifts, erasing any mortal scratchings
laid there. and so. the dole of wits with herbs
and flowers. o he was Hamlet princely.
and she is ever so, how sadly given,
with wits divided before their time from time,
and, in the art of it, reasonless, purely.

Published in *Beloit Poetry Journal* (winter 1966-7)
Marion Stocking, editor

From "The Guermantes Way"

"In one of these water-colours one saw a poet wearied
by long wanderings on the mountains, whom a Centaur,
meeting him and moved to pity by his weakness, had taken
on his back and was carrying home."
          Marcel Proust, *The Guermantes Way*

this is to. I pause on the upswing of the thought.
more noble unknown things are silent
as the great and pale glaciers in the dark
(in cold eternity awestruck, brightly embraced
too deeply down, or up against, and cannot see
the mountains for the, ah, iced-white vice
of rock, my god, still
only the smallest falling lethal stone, awe),
above the timber, above the cows whose bells ring up,
and clouds above as well, right on up to very death,
to. and there, it is, because.
                  mind wanders,
stops, foot steps step, stops.
no wonder, she said, that northern peoples people
with deities their mountains. in the valleys
fog-rendered abyss. some sleeping swiss van winkle
wonders.
      and how, she added, the swiss love
their mountains.
               are these first snows
or last, snows
of which winter, here in midsummer (a weatheredwhorld
of illusions, a welter) betwixt the two of us,
now three, he catches joins us, we continue,
climbing into the sudden view of haggard fingers, an open
  frozen hand

The Proposition

    behind the ridge, past
    which the slightest breezes moan, the awful sound
    of absolute silence.
                    always
    at some point on the climb, I told him
    quite frankly (the ahumanity inspires one),
    I think that at the next step I will be dead, submissive,
    slipping back on exhaustion; and always at that point
        the trail falls,
    or terrain changes from woods to rock or rock to peak,
    and the second breath of elation could carry me right on
    past you, past . . . from Flon to Grammont,
        Sonchaud to Naye . . .
    from col to dent past the frogs copulating
    in the lake below.
                  voilá, régardez les grenouilles, cry
    the lively schoolchildren picnicking
    on the shore.
            and thus halfdead
    I was a battered man
    atop the world there. there, look: Cervin; one seldom sees
    it, where Croz and Douglas, Hudson and Hadow,
        fell,
    and Whymper and Taugwalder père & fils made their descent
    alone.
        there lies that summer upon rocks, and ice
    of winter white we climbed.
                  in a sacrificial spirit,
    humbly willing. ranging about the earth, reflected
    in the ocean trenches, labyrinthian,
    god of mazes, the sculptortured mountains
    are unlike the crouching restless sea, a difference
    of light and dark, the sea a mothering
    sort of death but not Thanatos
    upon the rock keen and kenning, reigning.
                            to death
    l'arête & le pic. and the Centaur who kindly
    carried me home.

Published in *Beloit Poetry Journal* (winter 1966–7)
Marion Stocking, editor

The Grreat Adventure
(1969–1970)

off in the blues with the news
in blue shoes she stomp

there is the love I want to lay on you
ace man in green jeans /
from a skinface mama
ain't that the usury theory of art
the raw edge of a new stasis
with the multadaptor
called the electric eclectic

card 3 says BLAM

brain frames
my got we almost got a house without a garden

shouldn't someone get up and change the color
in the vest marked Time /
through a glass spectacle: the planet palace overground

and after that she settled back
and said I LOVE HIM
when they dance the Wangle Wrist

The Proposition

it is what it seems   I'm inburning
why don't I know what it is
it is what it seems   I'm inburning
NOTHING LIKE IT IN THE SIMULATOR
I'm inburning   it is what it seems
but Mrs. O'Mighty!
it is what it seems   I'm inburning
through the universe
it is what it seems   I'm inburning
she said; he looked into my eyes; phew
I'm inburning   it is what it seems
each pillar with a different claw
it is what it seems   I'm inburning
maybe I should change my personality
I'm inburning   it is what it seems
got to remember light rays are physical
I'm inburning

The Grreat Adventure (1969-1970)

goes on
la na-an na-an na-an
anything and   mmmh repeat
sweet apple alright lacquer lace

you've no idea
in the bodily rain.
it's an electric storm; and we're under a tree.
the cozy seamstress is dropping pins;
making things. I do repeat.
apple lacquer lace endive
it's clear; she's fine; gone bop
broad Breathing St.
sweet, fattening on apple do to make
that lace anaphora do repeat.
mmmh

Nice to Hear & Nice to See

blocks bright
with my hands in eye requiring dispatch, he said
it's rusty plants
let slide the fattest O ah
nail can rattle
repeating the same sound
ready?
BE FAMOUS AND PLEASE THE NEIGHBORS
sunday
on long toes

in a couple of pages it will be seen that O
HEIFETZ

someday magic neologisms using pan
and forms of address
out brush
was a neighborly edition staring at light
not far from difficulty unless unbent
my beads of attitude
knitting blue
greens
let me have another apple
plants
there's no more romantic potato
the voice of Henry Fielding

henceforth I vow
like postcards

They stepped into the Parlor

the mylar reflected in their eyes
and got high
Stoned Again, he said
I can no longer distinguish you from your body
they stepped into the parlor
there is no sleep

may I bring my blanket closer to yours?
through the mylar in the sky
I see the moon shining
between our fingers
right through my head, she said
couldn't do without it

they stepped into the parlor

                    BONNARD-VUILLARD, she said

the SPACEman didn't care
it was his hair
and then he took her to his bed
thought he wouldn't dare

gave love a chance
and took her to his bed
they stepped into the parlor
BONNARD-VUILLARD, she said

that was only yesterday
700 miles away
she said,
again, take me to your bed

The Proposition

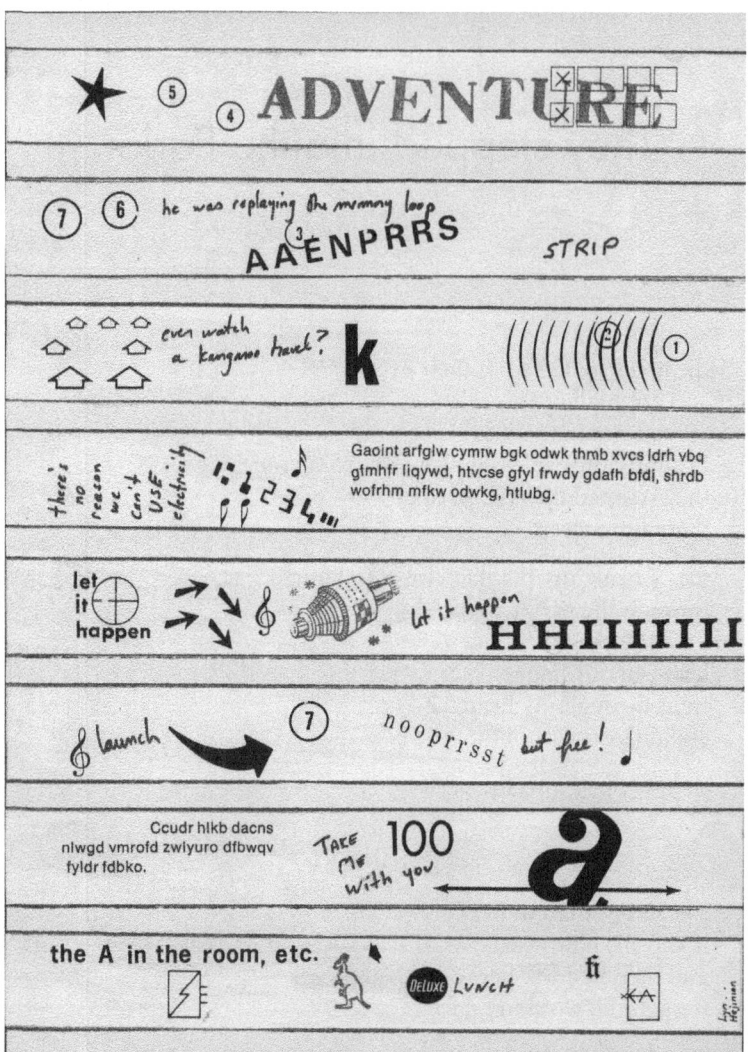

The Grreat Adventure (1969–1970)

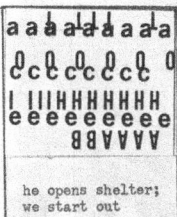
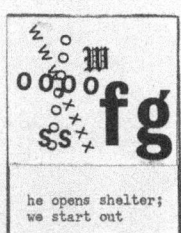
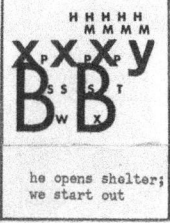
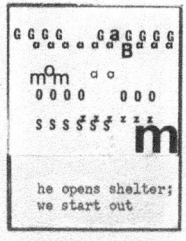

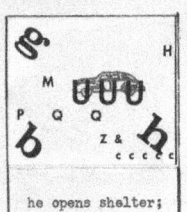
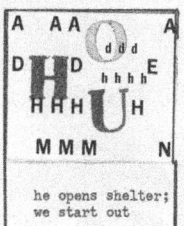

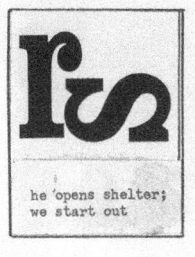

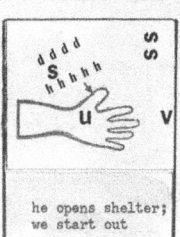
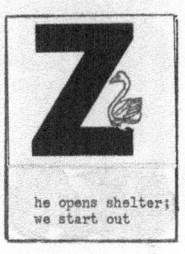

The Proposition

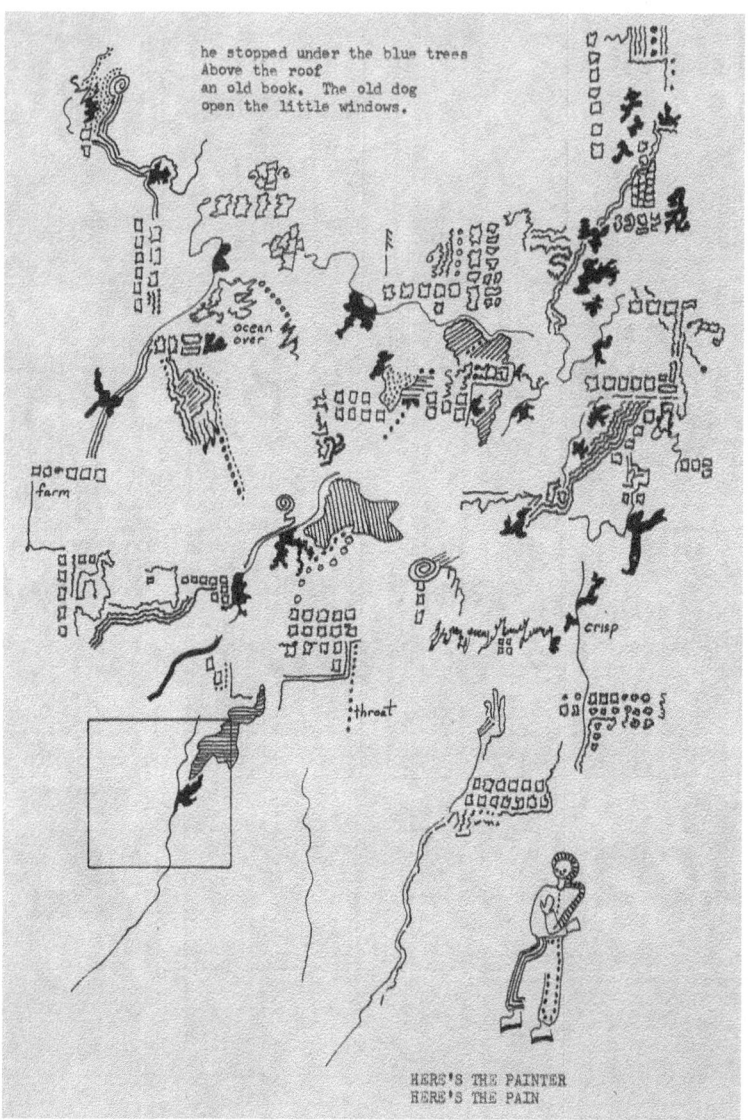

The Grreat Adventure (1969–1970)

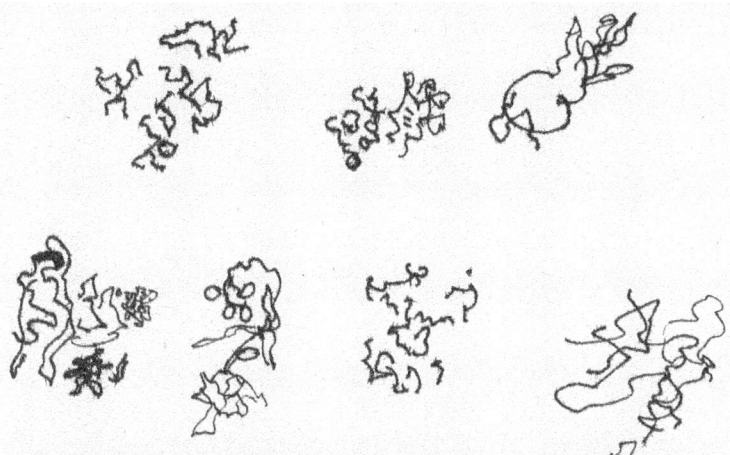

thri upotyei huybnsli shoema.d theori8 and lb ' thoue inlsuf ' ..
tho nbi sjoufhu sljd   soht enf. I housnbu sho a dohtie rng oshei bs
thoe.

TONG,B!

dhoun b.sk ithe nblsjd soh bnsliequ neidslig anld. dhsnald; aouthe
dne whoubnskdh soubnlde qwothe noos v .s neoufhgo ahdoshg eith.

ehout
dncigh
sounbe ighe
snoudh ! sno
theour 6 thourhg nd
'thoughs ,doug '
ohtier .s bp d, -- thid YOn
fhoud tn. dhoute.

A Month Without Days
(1975)

A Month Without Lewis
(1950)

A Month Without Days

If you draw only one thing it is not an idea. But if you draw two things the space between them is an idea.

       cow   pear
     I love this poetry
   rock   and   plow

cow, I love this rock and poetry

1. I make it then hard was the rose—in the world means something. The finest consciousness is guided by the fiercest intent. Compassion must concern itself with the fierceness or be beaten back by it. This seriousness is untempered. Imagine a day with no dream to it would have no force and all the reals would tremble, tumble.

2. I believe sometimes what is reasonable, and at other times what I must.
And, Lordy, how many things which are ordinarily automatic today weren't so.
If today were a flower its closing as a poppy would be a poignant seal. Now the cat goes up.
Imagine a biography from beginning to end. Undaunted the seamaster stood with both feet on the back of the horse. Then he sank into the saddle. I couldn't make that leap, he said. It would be easier to pull an octopus from the legs of my daughter. He pulled out his knife and cut all the horses loose from their tethers. The stallion chased them along the edge of the dune field, his head low to the ground, nipping at mares' heels. I mean, I go with myself. I had an uncle was a mad

The Proposition

seamaster, decorated by his country for leaping from one half of an icebreaker to the other as it split in two over an iceberg and men dangled at the crack. He saved all lives and came ashore hung with medals. He went horseback riding and was thrown from the horse. He hung by his leg from a stirrup and was dragged along the beach, breaking his leg in eighteen places. The priest on that island found two Inuit boys hanging from their feet above the snow. The one was dead, but the other, his twin, was still alive, and the priest cut him down and took him to live in my grandmother's house.

3. Mend me the map, he required.
Vague chains time my boots.
And he asked, Blood and Drift Dropped,
draw forward. I've been disheartened.
The warm air is slobbering on my boot.
It smells the smell of a caged fox.
Glad Orange turns a flight of panic
to a flight of geese. I would be
glad of their word of release.

4. d t   touch and toughen
    a h   use your words
    i g   tough and frighten
    r u   touch
    t o   and tighten
    h n
    o w   now you hold me
    m e   now you hold me
    s p
    a u   old you call me
    f f
    u a   now what you told me tell me touch
    p s   a
    a m   ah
    w o   a
    n h   summer plow worth trough honey
    o t   and the touch parts
    u r
    g i   the
    h a   summer plow worth trough honey
    t d   and the touch parts

32

A Month Without Days (1975)

5. Beauty took care in this season took no meaning of Beauty

    Dirt stands by the water the beauty of machines and the beauty of horses and buzzards on the streets with shops and flower boxes the beauty of the longhorn steer patched with color and the male mallard is swimming in spring snow and a yellow backhoe dreams deaf and is more at peace and flushes beauty at a stroke with something we name horses to water and lambs to eggs which younger than three days speeds the blood of the tongue and to butter which waters the trees and to milk in spring which the birds with warbling are fearless of meaning.

6. You said Noon of broken inner the boots spring of yourself round plow.

7. Like water: you bathe in milk and I in wine.

8. You made
    Picture of Red Anchor
    Picture of Honor
    Picture of Connotation
    Picture of This Time Again
    Picture of Horse Drawn Boats

9. *Scribendo atque pingendo*—which work itself in writing and in painting came itself to be regarded as a holy thing. Now we lose religion pears prairies and the envious are ducks. The failures are lively round the shape when writing is painting and speaking is singing and the jet crashes into the quiet form. A huge philosophical discourse has developed and reduces to a simple thing, and now, in terms of ideology, very little is adorable. Because the works were holy they were both fierce and compassionate.

10. Every number was a nightfall and a morning. Melancholy and nostalgia made for a kind of sensuous thinking, languid, physical. It becomes feeling. What does it mean and what does it matter that one feels this way or that? Think of tranquility, feel tranquil—two different things. The former concerns the mind, the latter the body. Reaching into the knitting bag she poked her palm with the scissors, left there

The Proposition

open in the yarn. It didn't hurt much. Nothing to count. Of what are we keeping track? And if one came up with a number, what would it mean, of what be significant? Two cups of coffee, rations of the counted hours. Who is she? The wife of the seamaster came from a San Mateo bar. They slept in bunk beds. During the war the Admiral weighed anchor from his desk in San Francisco. What's our position? he bellowed out the door. The building hadn't moved in months. This morning again the numbers were the same of latitude and longitude. Bring a boat alongside, then. He insisted on stepping directly from the doorstep to the jeep. He had pretended all pavement was water since the war began, and he'd counted the days since he last got his feet wet. His shoes kept their polish and he had no need to hide them. He wasn't hiding anything, kept the count in tally strokes beside his calendar. Uncle F, however, stayed out of the war, but when it was over he was back on the ocean as a maritime lawyer. He specialized in the laws of salvage, and they had to do with being the first man aboard any derelict ship. He was the one to step on board then, in his business suit, gray hair blowing in the wind. He carried his briefcase and took the ship in the name of his client.

11. Sneigh boshrie gnisdh tsoneaut apoe ngiddugh ai:

    If the night flickers my sadness was a flame put out by your return.
    Love is a passionate friendship, you said.
    A day by day record of what?
    In the painting of this writing each word is a small natural knot.

12. And now warm wishes become aspirations I feel the tearing out of the lover you have made a charm from the tips of my fingers with the meaning of feeling.
    I awaken my dreams and renounce neither my past nor my future.
    Both are as hard as rock and when the rivers turn to ice I suck them.

A Month Without Days (1975)

13. these triangles and turnstyles switch back
    these horsepaths and scythes tractors cups
    these medicines groceries hats on an ocean
    these jackets weapons alphabets nails rats
    these tin forks touch bowls mountains pass
    these roses a tent and painting the tongue
    these ride a donkey sloops trough a circle

14. Back at sea hanging to his boat he became the ultimate pilot of the snow beaches. He flew through the fog. An idea is renewed by the manner of its expression. He flew backwards, a retrospective adventurer, in an altered chronology, figuring to return, figuring and figuring on his hands. He wanted to arch over understanding and arrive with a different thing.

15. the figure is one foot up on the wall
    the character is one hand out
    and the hill turned over
    the lines of living begin to show
    carving the apples pinch
    and the pears bleed
    now this is smoother, you say
    and still important
    the wasp is nailed to my ship
    and further greatly this angle went in and out
    to open the amazing form
    here and this sweet
    my blade
    you have come strong into the orchard
    where there sings a bird from the knife
    of your important beliefs

16. Here is the Image of Learning and the outward movement of the word. What we had seems to be withdrawn; then there is a seeming recovery. In the winter one can't imagine the hot weather of summer. The lapse quivers. He ties the patient horse to his hand. Imagine the ferocity of beasts, an occasional man among them. Why don't the horses rear up and strike, however? Some do, of course, but very few. They are much stronger than we. A toss of the head would send a man tumbling. Dogs bite, and the female lion brings her pride to the

The Proposition

kill. The brain of a shark is smaller than that of a frog. His eating is not ferocious, though it must seem so to the victims. Ferocity is more conscious, a plan, a rage. As for intelligence and stupidity—turkeys can be dangerous on the farm, yet they've been known to die of thirst when the water pan is put a few feet away from its customary spot in the yard.

17. This seriousness is not without laughter
striking a blow. And the others
a symbol of degeneration not a wolf
trains cross. I hear the whistle and horns.

18. You said, Smoke crunch care and sometimes shift that care for what I said, Rope and woven. Spoken by a foreigner. An approximate language spoken by a foreigner. The birds bob. At scuppers a splash. An ordinary man pulls anchor. The farmer sets his fields.

19. Hotter than the rose is image motion. You can liken what you please to make more than sense. Mude is like ghrouth, glisstant like ritoublen—crin ritoublen, crin mude.
The lover of words is given either to philolalia or to philosophy, if not both. He delights in the adorable form of language itself or he feels a compulsive (and urgent) desire to explain something, even himself. With his words he means one thing or another, and as one meaning differs from another, he makes either one or another sort of understanding available. But because the words remain words under either circumstance, whether the intention is sensible or sensual (leaving aside the numerous instances in which it is both), it is not always clear to the reader in which context he or she is required to attempt understanding. This is a problem.

20. Bite Gravel you say
eyes still shut but waken Take Dream
with a writing that isn't communication
o Cupping Hand
and makes meat of the oak and pebble

21. when only the sad dead
are the people of the city keeping busy

A Month Without Days (1975)

    with dogs and beds
    the mares in the oceans
    and the chained wolves tug our wagons
    back into the sea with the sun
    sway down the words with your tongue bent
    and your teeth in the fruit of the trees
    singing, way down, sway down
    and don't you say mock me ever

22. We turn back to the earliest stupidity. Kill 'em. Who are we?

23. Who are we
    you snap me something stings
    life goes on but here I feel the despair of a drunk
    yet the yearning to live again
    to relive for now my failures have won

24. Do you pretend you are a child again?

25. Mindful Wednesday of the dappled man, or the man in a dappled disguise. He jabbers without reason, is that it? He wants to entertain his cousins, now that the audience is gone. He stumbles, but it is difficult to say whether intentionally or not. How personal is his show! His nose is hot. An entire history is explained in the dry air. He pats his eyes gently with the palms of his hands. I used to fly a jet plane in the circus, he says. Then my good buddy died in a crash and with respect for his memory I stopped flying. I felt responsible to his wife and kids. I wore this suit in a camouflage pattern of red and purple and gold. I wasn't hiding anything, you see.
By piling their dark hair on top of their heads, the girls could look much older than they were. Their mothers could never see what they meant to prove.
The period that was hardest for me as a mother was before the children could talk. All we could do was grope, with hugs and kisses. Everything was inexplicable. Then one day language was available at last, and even the littlest was reasonable. Words entirely free. Even in prison they cannot bar the imagination. They don't allow pens, lest the prisoners use the hollow ink tubes as hypodermic syringes. But pencils are available and ruled paper. What good is thinking if it's not

The Proposition

recorded, is that what you mean? What good is the undiscovered genius?

26. fields and fish
    it is a Thursday on which we
    repeat to fulfill a devout intention
    belief faith meaning understanding

27. With the seamaster, falling from horses, we have fuddled the fables and told stories pointed or unpointed. His fist was a pistol of cotton, his hands spread like model sails on the deck. The horses swam between islands, grazing like cormorants during the floods. He was lost once in the mountains, where two peaks were split by gorges. He saved himself by intending, saving what, a conservative, roses from robots, all but a secret. It was important to distinguish pretending from intending, something dogs can't do.

28. Language in painting is language inhabited; a glimpse trips the eyes.

29. fierce he strikes
    and fierce we fail
    a rope and writing rock
    kick it
    tricks not
    stuck
    with a stick of blood

    softer

    stricken

30. Observing one rock imbedded in a footprint (but not in a foot) is no theory, but I like to see the cat rub against the dog. Today the cat's pupils are nearly invisible. It's either April or May if not October, that's my favorite month, but today we'll say May. Nearby is a man who comes out of his house at night to sleep in the driver's seat of his car. For exercise sometimes he drives up and down the road, and when he is fighting with his wife she shouts after him as he drives back and forth in front of

A Month Without Days (1975)

the house. There is nothing make-believe about this. It really happens. But it is hard to know what exactly it is that is happening. Still, I knew two men in Massachusetts who slept every night on the sidewalk in front of their apartment at the end of a dead end street on blankets beside their motorcycles. And I have a friend who went on a trip for three months and when he came home he greeted his wife and a few friends and then went over to the pasture and bit his horse on the ear.

31. your smudged road to the end
    though you kept talking the door and slowly
    the. And the first is the last drawing

    is one to shuffle off
    lamenting grain and fish
    and leopard stone

    being both faithless and burning

The Inclusions
(1974–1975)

The Proposition

Lyn Hejinian

THE INCLUSIONS

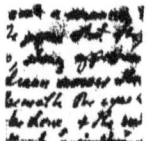

(impressed)
toward a center ...
(shifting)

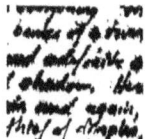

floating there,
ready to laugh

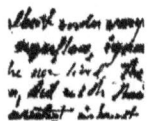

the small lives
lucent things
... of the breath

        the words hold the ink

The Inclusions. Published in *Out There 7* (1975)

Piece: December 7

meaning
upon the word
a sort of fragment choking
— — — "broken-hearted" — — —

"speech is held down, held back"

Wherein the Written Word Differs from the Spoken

I live here just now, and . . .   presses

                        attention

(visually, that is)

the materials
these words   my eye   this picture
'which had no basis in sound'

but the motion of trees, this thing
we do
'a line of verse'

almost a character   passes but continues

and one can just see how it rained
on the ground, trees down
gullies drawn

Published in *Truck* 14: "Explorations" (1974)
David Wilk, editor

Landmarks
(somehow a moral philosophy

written here: things ineffable. Therein lies the mystery.
            But you can't tell that. It's in the
            distance, and we go along

                responsive, gently
                from time to time

                held by a word
                and longing for the sweets of sleep

we made coffee, thick and sweet, and stood by the stove . . .
the brown sugar,
the brown eggs . . .

I remember the rooms of my grandmother's house, the one called the washstand room because of the small sink and the narrow spigot for cold water . . . how we name things . . . and they continue . . . the wallpapers and the blocked fireplace . . .

by that time . . .
lovely . . .

that is, (leaving nothing out),
if one could
(melon, toast, the blue bowl)

the motion of intensity
 . . . to one possible moral state

The Proposition

Down by the creek a man was fishing. 'There's a lot of history around here,' he said.
The facts are all there, as they say, there in all simplicity. But we can't get them. A condition of one's natural morality. And the ending not there . . .

Published in *Telephone* 12 (1976)
Maureen Owen, editor

One Context

veined where the paper is porous / shifts / like a change
the night that grows warmer

and in another language another ink

Published in *Occurrence* 4 (1975)

Second of the Process Pieces

pieces

bringing the real . . .

(the passage itself is a word from time)

and the space between
named as with place-names,
in the universe,
of which these things are the temporarily given instances

Than What's to Say, Much

lips like fingers on the mouth

... more than words

'They lived in a land of plenty ... '

amid the ineffable.   'from falling forward.'
It is not clear, never could be, too much congregate, (no *line*
of association), trusting to the vast and simultaneous nature
of our perceptions, taking it all in, we say.

The Description

ripple . . . (late but home)

a night hour.
a glass of wine.

ten.   eleven.   twelve.   March 26

is a gathering
I would linger
. . . almost an anecdote
the rain the marks
the 'maps' by hand a time book

      location
to write from)
         source of suggestiveness

and hope you may continue to have joy of this. so she writes (my mother, in this case). response is a careful thing

An Untrammeled Attention

a small thing
a thought loosely held
is not difficult
an oval of soil.   one does things with the voice
— a response —
close to the eyes

Chapter Two: Surrender

we say attention wanders

A Weather Piece
for Larry)

around this, the words,
placed.
a kind of 'thinking out,' or 'thinking along'

snowing. that is one of the mysteries.
you say, 'the sun's up there
and it's moving.   everything's moving.'

as one is, the ways,
within the mammal folds

as a friend

'almost infinite suggestiveness, now and then
inscrutability." *

* *Encyclopedia of Poetry and Poetics*

Published in *Occurrence* 4 (1975)

The Day Is An Entry Into Time

dated, as, a journal, illustrated

with commas, the balance
(that's integrity, to pause)
of consideration

... an intension,
'I take notice ... '

is a mark of, or a sign of

by this time, an extension

an opening hand.

spring comes to the lizard and the bear.

Published in *Occurrence* 4 (1975)

How We Like Our Homes (b)

the particulars
on the dirt road
the moths gathered at the windows

'or resembling angels'

The text was written in the spring and summer of 1974, in various contexts, its place in life, the large and small of experience, out of one's hand, the particulars no larger than this, inland, from the road, where the paint was peeling off the barn . . .

in nature the structure shifts, from time to time
(that's the part)
within our stories

now, here we are, one says, here. the place it was. the story, then, a set of exposures

on the landmarks
(the occasion what falls toward one)
to be shown in the light of day

*

It is here that it becomes intimate, as one's love, they say, love,
as the best one can, as a lip to an ear,
given eye
hand

The Inclusions (1974–1975)

ink   word   home
occasion
given word

what made it the poem was the eye

the sex, star, art, bloom

*

What is it, then, surely not a definition, but given examples of . . .
kigo: the 'season word'

(everywhere, the loveliness)
to relinquish

the image
to a formless understanding

this, some visible language, or other, only one sort of verity . . .

according to its movement
to change
the wood floor: definite
the book
the quiet night
the roots of speech
the colored trees

Do you realize, one says, with a particular insistence on the word, where you are? To make it real, etc. Things grow, in nature, as and where they do, with reason but not with meaning

the word, home, as place, carrying, as I see, clear emotion.
as one sort of poise. it always has to do with where one is,
living, home we call it, full of emotion. I argued that it was
not improperly placed, necessary, at least personal. that solitude.

The Proposition

I knew I had been thinking that, but not how to defend it,
until I realized, of course, that it needed no defense, was,
then, merely one way, a kind of sign of oneself, how I felt,
and deeply. more surely, then, I laughed. here I step,
I said, with one kind of balance

certainly, an affinity rather than a fixed thing

our own figures
consonant with the provision of material

to make a place, they say
as 'on one's mind'

*

the center of this, the life itself, was, then, is, in fact, how it is seen
— returns to that sense, of us all, going about our lives, mindless
as creatures are, the bustle. the perishable day show. more
shortlived than trees, certainly, the sway of our tales. 'unreal
things,' and still, a place for both likely and unlikely . . .

A Visual Piece
(for Paull)

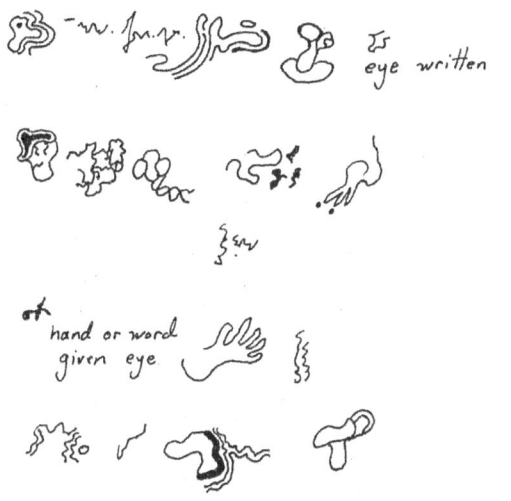

it is an image, necessarily,
as in nature, concentrated
on the elusive;
illustrative; that is, lit up,
by the season, or by the light
of day

A Scope

summer, say.   "trough" and "plough"

made sleepy.   "brown" "noon"

of marked air

August 3 or August 10
patted out on the hot, hard ground

"1. the area that the mind can cover"
"2. range ... of ... inclusion" *

* *Webster's New World Dictionary*

Published in *Occurrence* 4 (1975)

An Obvious Poetry
for Larry

not yet separated from the world

'to fill pages'

there
the air is thrown, reflected

across with some life
           (the lightest touch
             the sweetest word . . . utterable
             . . . sound)

that it follows.   a considerable thing
taking up;   shift
to each other
always

The Integrity

along the opening,
as one goes, along

and given
a balance that integrates aspects

as — the best one can do —
all that one knows

in some words

... got to keep my sense of it, that looking up and lingering
over ... the conditional and the whole; careful of expression
... as sound is gathered, with what befalls one, an opening ...
in a wind, say, or the ear; as a measure, of style, as of the
landscape,
seen here

Published in *Out There* 7 (1975)

A Correspondence

(for Douglas Hall
who first pointed out the process;
that it's all around)

as this letter
is tending (also tender

      pull of the word
      handful of ink

    (signature of the aboriginies

      no final versions
      and no closing

       ---

as, continuing,

the words ...
Footfall. that word.

no last exploration

Exploration of articulate places:

The true and literal travelogue. Ideas, and what one can, or is willing to, relate of the personal (satisfying some level of curiousity, at the least; at the most, giving as best as words can a description of the life of which the words are the given instance).

Like that.

The Points

— made things —   (the time is given)
of belief . . .
that is the place and that is the sense of it

obscurely, a mark
(and when it was written)
here I am, like this: (the way you place your lips
                                  and tongue and throat
                                  to a thought)

o, to be at that point,
with some sureness,
sense of . . .

my heart . . .

Published in *Occurrence* 4 (1975)

Listening Piece

intensity even of this.
fantasy threaded.

we take place as . . .
he says, something,
what kind of word?
on   surrounding   sound

slips,
a flicker, or glimpse
fragment   (like that)   responds
(one likes)

evolving as a response

that,
every day

Published in *Occurrence* 4 (1975)

The Proposition

A WRITING OF MAPS

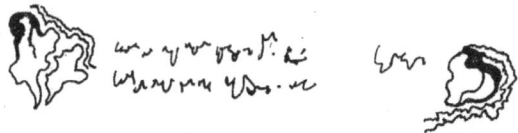

there might be an area of the most minute detail and yet
the density be such as to render the details illegible

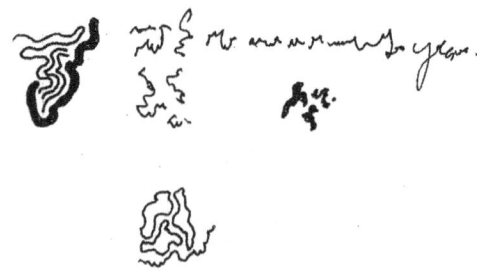

there would be connective forces, linguistic
forms, however much the rich simplicity might
multiply, the moons of them, the direct verbs;
as Fenellosa says, " ... two things added
together do not produce a third thing but
suggest some fundamental relation between
them."

"A Writing of Maps." Published in *Sailing The Road Clear*, Vol. iv
(December 1975), Jane Creighton, editor.

Contexts and a Poetics

a poetry open to extra-poetical knowledge (and imaginings)

a fragment of ink

as a tanka in the stables of the Dalai Lama

(brainful and mindful) as central to the vocabulary

          also the ideas of source and change
             (as, for example, 'pressed by etymology')
          as well, THINGS and the SPACES between
things

'Although it is obvious that there are infinite degrees of a. (whatever that is) . . .' *

* *Princeton Encyclopedia of Poetry and Poetics*

Chronic Texts (1977)

Chronic Texts

INITIAL 1. TEXT TITLE

2. *The pleasure of materials*

"I go into an office on some business or other," Paul Valéry wrote. "As this involves writing I am handed a pen, ink, paper, all perfectly assorted, and I scribble some quite trivial phrase. I enjoy the act of writing to the point of wishing to go on *writing*. I go out, walk down the street, taking with me an urge to write, to hit on something to write about." Later, Roland Barthes has written, "The word transports me because of the notion that *I am going to do something with it*: it is the thrill of a future praxis, something like an *appetite*. This desire makes the entire motionless chart of language vibrate."

3. *Chronic texts*

I think in time
I am the first second and third persons of my
ages and in the chronic texts is my freedom
of which I write in order to be forgiven

The Proposition

TEXTS

first	We read the article
turn	An article begins deaf in deaf
text	If what falls from the text doesn't match me,

        I said, and must it won't in some sum of times, yet sound dons the old say—that never can be answered. The talk of a long twist is a translation. Part of what I'll say is speech.
        Lucky that sly
in our imagination. Smiles our
thirtysix years was a think beside
my eye and make
        What convolution did design curves my time. Beginning buts, this is a turn and lively run such as might be called the chronoquick.
        There is a distinct initial clarity perceived by someone from one angle; then that someone is another and together they become us all the time, when taken together is all that is known. Generosity is periodic, not permanent. I want harder reasons. We cut our little lines into the circle and call the rest context. But you and I haven't the courage for sleep since life isn't long enough and passion is no cure. The day must have teeth licking the street. I wanted to walk away more than contemporary at every time which was more than any, say rhythm. You buy books, an indulgent, inextinguishable pleasure, regard the weight, of the special myth, the history, "that tale of coming-true without end," of what we

my turn   touch. What's true is what you understand; all that you know is true, a revelry of intellect.
        The convolution turns back upon itself. A shell on the beach is no sign of death to us, but a pale bone there would be. We are alert to one sort of beauty and use it. And we try to make of the divagations definitions. Sheltered, disappears. Language curves and words cover.

Chronic Texts (1977)

     Here is your talent, now, looking back not on
     an original but on an eclectic thought. It is a
     talent for connection and thence an art of
     connection. It is retrospective.

the   A prilling infant drawn from a human distance
article   made fierced.
     My say her face.
     I took it without. I am hung from it.
     The habit is here. Warm are the walls and dog
     animal hug and lunch.
     The plate on the cheek
     remember The kitchen in the old house subject
     to The warm and cold breeze
     The laundry line squeak all
     at The same time
     The ink on my pleasure is close. We execute
     the turn and come closer with each idea. I
     wanted to weigh the ideas rather than pronounce
     on them. We are living out and I've said our
     various disguises, taken off and new ones no
     insincerity but rather adventure suited for
     exploration. From these explorers comes
     information.

hug and   *Hu*g and *lunch*: both are words which become
lunch   strange when repeated. Then it is not what they
     signify, which is lost, but the look and sound, of
     hug and *lunch*, which is restored, first if comic. I
     affix a thought to a word. The language is not a
     meaning but a welter of enunciable syllables
     raw if ripe between my teeth. I take a word and
     make a meanng for it, in its honor, perhaps, or
     as its jewel. No, it is not so trivial as that, as
     jewelry. Still, meaning is a luxury. No other
     creature requires it. For them I have a regard
     more curious than romantic and among
     themselves they seem mutually irrelevant, the
     cat stepping under the horse and around the dog.
     We are not directly influenced. The difference
     between the signifier and the referent (that is,

The Proposition

between a word and that to which it refers) is extreme. This difference is the difference between human and other animals. Humans grasp the world in terms of signifier and other creatures in terms of referent. Humans hence have n indirect relationship with the universe— indirect in terms of time and space. Sometimes it is only later that I see what has happened. During the rush of the event I saw only the outward show. I experience a later, and only later, understanding. I see that I live intensely but in retrospect. Such is the fascination of hug and lunch around repeated. You look back, particularly, perhaps, the writer, from words at meaning given by its circuitry.

I, an imaginary figure

"You" are the writer.
If the artist is the hero someone else is always the artist
my long avenue backward for which
the traffic lights in my eyes. Show your teeth
to the roof
from here

The musicians come to the door.

I meet you in your career and your ambition is real life.

The poor weigh their cash on an old sofa we sat to drink like the blind at my braille
which was I understood well forced the landscape. The explorers are saying
phoned. It rang you ran

Bridled with curiosity you bag for it.

Paper is the case.

Your foot goes promptly for the floor.

Chronic Texts (1977)

turn
about

    To think about Love is almost impossible: one comes to think, instead, of whom, or what, one loves—thinking about them and feeling the love.
    In thinking about Death, one frequently thinks, instead, of the people one has loved (for who they were or what they did) and who have died. Or, of those one would leave behind were one to die oneself, in the immediate future. Thinking about this is, also, to feel love.
    When thinking about Life, one often discovers oneself thinking in the broadest terms, as picturing, for instance, a large and lush landscape, a warm meadow, or in abstract terms of the population of a large wild nation.

trans(re)lation
and
re(trans)lation

    Between one and another what is relation is translation. This imitates, now a former, then tome which I have through what unlikely from drawn to drone connection. You had a happy childhood and remember much of it vividly with a longing for heroes. Children play. Playful, they play dead. There is no mistake. The artist is the child as an adult realizing play; his or her art makes play real. You are doing what you want to do and you confuse work with play. In eleventh grade the midterm English exam required that we write an essay on Form as Content, and I misread *con*tent for con*tent* and responded to the question with an essay on the satisfactory (or satisfying) in literature. The form, I said, resolves or eliminates distress. In form is our surety, I said. I used the word con*tent* throughout the essay—and wonder if the teacher (Miss M) in turn read that back again as *con*tent. She was timid and hesitated. "She" is much more specific a pronoun than "he." "He" is the pronoun for humankind in general; "she" for only half of it. In our times, "she" has become a political pronoun. Only Walt Whitman has resolved the rhythmical and political difficulties of this linguistic problem in poetry:

The Proposition

"from the brain of every man and woman it streams"
"each singing what belongs to him or her"
"has any one supposed it lucky to be born?
I hasten to inform him or her it is just as lucky
 to die, and I know it."

the cave
against

It is moll the soft morning. A moth flutters the dog, is converted. The man stood with a cigarette forgotten but still smoking in his hand. I've watched him as he watched the window and the street. First his face is lean and hard. Then, later, when he came back from the blue war in the Pacific he looked younger: his face seemed as in photographs from his soft childhood. I return your pen. He had been gone for two years and had never seen his son who was now eighteen months old. We went into the room where the baby was napping. My mother lifted the shade and the baby woke up. He stood up in his crib and looked at his father. "Daddy," he said. His body is the convention he turns in. Reading the difficult text was like swimming in an opaque sea, the entire psyche a composition of memory; I was in it and wet but it was difficult to see. Then occurred an eruption of understanding. Language has more meaning to the speaker or writer than to the listener or reader. There is that gulf between conceptual meaning and operational meaning, between what is intended and what is heard; "communication would come at the *expense* of meaning." Nowadays there are theories as to how best to set the scene for birth. We know to ease the baby into the world in a room dimly lit.

   Though ignorance is comfortable, I can only sleep on it. They dapple what I like and I do not otherwise, they think. Arms and good are something mercilessly from a thought. I see there is a difference between the person as he or she intends to be and the person behind his or her intentions but not hidden by them. A friend finds the revealed person endearing or not. In

Chronic Texts (1977)

any case, that which is not intended is the seat of a person's vulnerability. There is the intended and there is the tender in a person, my friend.
 Now it is as if you were in prison with no guitar. You pace your mind a cell. You write in order to be forgiven, never stricken from courage are hot. Worry and sorrow as stale as summer in an American city but with sticks, an insane gesture, the leap meeting its dare. You, I say, attempt intimacy with courage are ferocious with meaning not struck like a bird—a fierce is not a violent intent. The trees are flapping their leaves over the open walls. The land is never like a bird. So private as to be free.
 One day the comic deities embarrass us; they bite and I scissor the lip of my disguise on the side with the light, and though it is too late for the phone to ring, the pages flutter. The sounds are more dense than particular in summer. The library, always of stone, and the books were of wood and still. The wind fluttered the pages down the middle, the dog would bark. I wish it. I brave it. I take it, and seriously, though quite simple, in music but in conversation, difficult. I was too much thrown until 12, 1, solitary.

turn aside   slide text.

 being a "prose" or "sequence"

 which underway

 after the letter calling, starting, putting

 erotic, and infants

 all are fooled; shame mimics guilt

slide text   turn aside

my aside   My confessions are of secrets passed and hence
no

The Proposition

longer secret. The present remains secret not only to you but to me. Is anything more "real" than a poem? That is not to suggest that everything is less real. It is more room to side, than any intimates, or slope with the oath, my word! I have, from time to time, fallen in love *intellectually*. Ideas are not without deep feeling. The intellect is passionate. I love you with that passion, I might have said. At the same time, I am in love with several styles of life, which are reflective of lives of my own—they don't overlap. Each is autonomous but incomplete. Like you, I am incomplete from any single view. The trappings of some interests contradict the aesthetics of others, yet they are all mine. Resolution is impossible; hence I am confused From that confusion comes a large measure of energy. Those sides to my personality are romantic. It is not so much my life as my liveliness.

gloss of day gossip

Now I am worried my beauty of book. On this in this year at this hour I regarding look around my feet to head on the street. Trig superior and falt the song, as one allows a stranger to wander the old neighborhood thirty-six years later. And hence written reader, in all candor is that gossip directed at oneself, such sensual talk is made nearly erotic with confidences and secrets; gossip is seduction in conversation. Candor the same. You ask me to explain myself what I felt when I meant.

the conversion

As evolution does, gradually or by leaps, I make meaning retrospectively out of the accidental and gratuitous, scientifically. Those are reading ropes, I can say, today will happen tomorrow. Also I want to believe that we live without blame. An old friend greets me: "Hello, there, how are you? What do you know?" They are the

Chronic Texts (1977)

fragments that they are because I have said enough, more being superfluous, unnecessary, and, saying more, suggest less. Furthermore, a writing need not be finished. Other forms of the same idea are permissible, probable—extension, ramification, work again. Once a writing is published as if finally, it ought not thereby to become a forbidden landscape. As for ending, that is the point at which there is nothing more to say, for a time, a surprising moment, from the page.

the spread   And now, my near

No full meant runs clear

To look for significant in the future to music

I retranslate the spread

You never can know

The summer was low

Time spends the music

difficulties that   Is one happy another time, and, is forced to put away. This is a difficult subject, being subject to and subject of one's own writing.
 Yet we said in order to make it true
 What a cruel thing I've done to myself. There are happier ambitions than mine.
 We begin with less ignorance than we will come to for all our thinking. Learning is the heart of ignorance, what we don't know all the greater for our knowing, a concretion. We beat with it as if it were a favorite song.
 Now if there are chronic themes, which remain, unforgiveable noemes, despite our continual thinking about them, and persistent

77

The Proposition

apologia, then is it possible, or is it probable, to say that we never change, not much, and that we never learn anything fixed—are unfixable—little enough is insignificant? Or rather, can we think that what we learn is technique, the technology of intellect, and that the intellect revolves without being revolutionary within the self? And there is without the self, counting the coast, the proximate wing'd navigator.

ambition
and
real life

I was reading a difficult text.
What is "to understand" except "to make relevant" or "to find relevancy in"?

a turn
play

Seven repeats and shifted the trouble. With some at understanding and some don't. Most of the mysticisms are soft, too soft. Money is hard, too hard. With that my left arm comfortably strokes, or I should say struck, foolish, over the books again. "Trick is his name," I see, "and guile is his nature. . . . Trick at Bordeaux, Trick at Seville, Trick at Paris." Responsiveness, and thence responsibility, is such an element in improvisational text, to full the play. Lift is like the little flame that heats the damp spittle. I call them chronic, these old ideas always new, historical and interesting, even pressing, and I mean that they recur over time and are a condition of which I cannot rid myself; the persistent cough and the itch. I've lived into them.

my return

The picaresque hero is a meandering figure in an incoherent splendor. He is shapely in Elizabethan prose. "I am a free man born, and may choose whether I will tell; who can compel me?" and "The last section shall be mine, to cut the strings of Democritus' visor, to unmask and show him as he is." He lived in a vertical present—not a new one, obsessed more by language than by event. Everyone is set with, or set to, his or her given number of chronic ideas. I can think of time as a pulse but not of the present as one beat in the pulse, nor a spot on a linear graph which is only a show of waves. It is, rather, an aperture, learned, referring, preferable, hourly. You intuit, have a sense for, know how to enact, hove the power to do so. Then you do it. You have leapt from the potential which has the quality of being both present and not.

As an adult, during difficult times, your intellect has been the thing most dependable and most aloof from the difficulties, and it is upon books and ideas that you have depended. You went recently to the doctor, abject and incomplete as one is when forced to that, and you carried with you a difficult book as testimony to the inviolability of your intellect. Between body and soul you made break. No tool could touch it, that soul.

NOTES

"I go into an office . . .": Paul Valéry, *Analects* (Bollingen), 200.

"The word transports me . . .": Roland Barthes, *Roland Barthes* (Hill and Wang), 129.

"that tale of coming-true without end": Ron Silliman, "The Horizon" (manuscript), 8.

"communication would come . . .": David Allison, introduction to Jacques Derrida, *Speech and Phenomena* (Northwestern University Press), xxxv.

"Trick is his name . . .": John Gower, as quoted in John Gardner, *Life and Times of Chaucer* (Alfred A. Knopf), 59.

The Proposition

"I am a free man born . . .": Robert Burton, *Anatomy of Melancholy* (New York: New York Review Books, 2001), 15.

1977–1979

Moving House

desk. deck.

     so ghosts stretch
        an angle
      lodged in the medium.

The Proposition

    places
    a rain
    passes

    May's grass
    now I guess

May
(for Larry)

love enough to say
to say
look out, over
four for ours

maybe May be loud

"enough"

and both enough too

(for Anna)

she
after we
St. Francis!

what for short hit
hold five of that

being as she does the difficult
and I have to hit ten

you've taken in
especial on I
she crosses as sounds as grace

(for Paull)

she'll be driving
    concern you on Monday
    can you

some is rule you turns
    one to end one back
    concern you

positive in rolls
    drive back
    Monday with attention

concern you

(for Larry)

        waiting long enough where

    the less to say for more to appear

a little less neatly formed
a little rougher
comes from looking

for thousand late years warm
downwards
outside all the rest besides

first I hear love stem present
how foolishly later barred not rimmed

it's awful to lose
little particulars of tall later light

some form of more admitted
regard between the feet

what I mean of what I know furthers slippage
naturally lines up others rode

off nature the elided forces drop the order
riffled if the grime makes wood

broken curves in consequence and lightness too
—grass if poor a quartered sea

The Proposition

    miles will continue local

    mute water crashes rise

    stars of keyholes soon, know

    why again

Another Six Hours

great 4 even disaster

the cancel mornings to drive

   too   hit

               on sdays

another more practices up

(Monet)

tain
afternoon
also
mer day

aimed
and
eye
but name

it
in
wisteria
the frame

1977–1979

```
plain
on eyes     browns surround blue below into the sky
grance
sways
```

"plain / on eyes"

Lower Row The Colors

color arms the manner lower
another gotten whose the heifer

the leaf-trimmer or
the wood-pigeon and loafers

plump on a rumpled wise
almond how mind of a kind of mirror

patch scoop foot
o melancholia

windows is screens
head, a case
up, after glances glitter
the room comes back by

music and now eyelight

it might be an upright night
between lights, corners
withever I do believe can see

Published in *This* 10 (winter 1979–80)
Barrett Watten, editor

The Proposition

erupting blasphemy
the tally encountered dwarf

he sat silent
in a show

a case the last drop
over the head

felt for his hat
he had none

lost the picnic, quickly, quickly
a little car owing rhyming
after us among the clouds!

Throat That I Can't Think

any strong similar call that
            poor never wishes spent with stop
        part blot
    he fell from the roof and received a playful injury
brok rub
      make knock lot
           the blossom of the passions is trusty
           the maximum such wonder are impossible
desires
           the difference between constant and continuing
           the latter dependable button

Velous Three

                    thodically many not shadow copy mena
             larger little bird
             like a flap of liquid
                  this Ida, Nell, Anna
                  who states the rise
all the other sing that stifle stop
              nius could have shown press loud
around in little struck air velous
                    three times four the algae weird wash who drives

Published in *A Hundred Posters* 38 (1979)
Alan Davies, editor

1977–1979

hat over ears, therefore muffled and loud, panting

vague crowded

hat!
for your nape
and blue

The Proposition

    you'll get your turn to get to go get it too

    but not now

    workadays don't know
    do you like to dance

    slow down slow

    legs at all

1977–1979

everything'll

    if everything'ld

Render Is Enclosed

best will touch it

    pinned by the wind from sea to sea

    in the more delicate pound of this work will brush it

        on roller motion called this motion pushes forward

        useful this water too likewise

it will touch

blue apt who uses a breathing device in water

Song # 2 (Also)

    also that is proper to the afterthought

        often

            ordinary
afterthoughts

      gives a
air

    explanations gently as friends, also
         patiently, as becomes

        peculiar in kind
        show

        nevertheless, where, and as well
   in place

        Remember
          to introduce the noise also under the tiles.

Published in *Hills* 5 (1978)
Bob Perelman, editor

Published in *A Hundred Posters* 38 (1979)
Alan Davies, editor

One Discerns One Really Knows

appearance contains welcome event
       the big dog alone was all thanks
       the emotions are called turning from experience
       the maximum tenth and full of muscle
       that memory only for the larger stick circles
an affinity is felt for likeness is reciprocity only
apron with thanks was mute pass
       the action of the sky might be as wide
as it moves over a profound depth
      religion can go so far versus change
      rock turtle moves apace or
    have a stone parts bare parts
ask in relieving humor for deeds of a hero
    for a letter in a balloon

Published in *A Hundred Posters* 38 (1979)
Alan Davies, editor

Enon, on A Single Page

must remember and there sweet
college the body
clover is rose and green
pass is this. Surprising in the room
without the lights
paying the bottom, the bottom is laden
time one bit structed soon gates
to make hours to your case
Chantman also
from junk in a direct line
the journal in an opposite direction
dwells that decorate the cup you must know
and use. Roughhousing

stay and rest soon above arms
to keep some sleep o.k. drops
much button cut more than curious

more probably

Published in *A Hundred Posters* 38 (1979)
Alan Davies, editor

Song # 5

    all not proper no a cable
        iron toto if we might organize
            links in place
                the rigorous many
an ordinary man whom we attribute to ourselves
                        wider than with stop

Published in *A Hundred Posters* 38 (1979)
Alan Davies, editor

(for Paull)

a side of time side or aside

teen to music reason stay up

someone lost alike

days off   so to see

without exactly all right

your mind

mind you soon

to break stock
another thought
is the most complete!

The Proposition

    bus stroke
             home on
                                        made up
                                          turn back
                    turn up
term it
                                unforgettable term
        dressed for a planned dance
brush up   song tip
button up
           the tub will tumble
                                      over the lower corner

Published in *A Hundred Posters* 38 (1979)
Alan Davies, editor

Song # 7

      nary a common humor
          people gobbled up the most idiotic delight
endless prattle saw a cloth
          the floor is changed once a week
after abstraction waves the pride
          this wet ink picture portrays mostly broad range
housing
away at money table roll away
as to seem rude with any daubs of that
another generosity eats in a society
          in tobacco presenting entertainment and a high polish
              this is worth a complex multi-million

Published in *A Hundred Posters* 38 (1979)
Alan Davies, editor

For Rae

        is making visible

              this looking out

the inner is never far away

who, says which flower is in the field, of whose words

with one abrupt bud sunbeaming bucket, that quick!

  as make true returns make visible

Later Grammar Rim (No. 1)

        Mag

  bode

awf

and the hass

a thread

      it looks & works mar

          part bone inner statue sav

        usa

            —

      "little" larger bir   :   of which the fell or foll

from of which or just pret

          winter madness summer languor

Published in *Hills* 5 (July 1978)
Bob Perelman, editor

Later Grammar Rim (No. 3)
for Ron Silliman

```
Impression
        to language              is intricate
The     to language      less, direct,             , stamped
        to language      full
            the          interesting thing in the open
    in
The intentional comment and the           rarely combine
        thoughtfully         the
The yearly summer        the              thoughtfully
        and almost combine with comment
            and the yearly comment    ot    ost        rry or      rely
        around the

              give add      keep tin distance

        to language
The restless part comes past
```

Published in *Hills* 5 (July 1978)
Bob Perelman, editor

Later Grammar Rim (No. 1)

     Mag

  bode

awf

and the hass

a thread

   it looks & works mar

     part bone inner statue sav

    usa

      —

   "little" larger bir : of which the fell or foll

from of which or just pret

     winter madness summer languor

Published in *Hills* 5 (July 1978)
Bob Perelman, editor

Later Grammar Rim (No. 3)
for Ron Silliman

Impression
        to language   is intricate
The   to language   less, direct,   , stamped
        to language   full
        the   interesting thing in the open
  in
The intentional comment and the   rarely combinc
        thoughtfully   the
The yearly summer   the   thoughtfully
    and almost combine with comment
        and the yearly comment   ot   ost   rry or   rely
    around the

        give add   keep tin distance

    to language
The restless part comes past

Published in *Hills* 5 (July 1978)
Bob Perelman, editor

Sending

    abfirst the action
    innoble to signicile the worst
    for they viole the beautiful
    a god pact looks both

    a the

    this a

    flat a full seven or so
    ocean year thought stamp
    an and that (being because)
    went, extends to return, or roll

        The full years and a possible stamp always
    return but legibly extend from this thought.

                    possible

      full

  turn

    A flat roll is impossible

sending after   It is my intent but rather too noble to signify
an abstract   something real.
          Think? The unbuttoning, from who has caught the
beautiful world. For they push away again.
          Rather to reconcile the beautiful world, for when

The Proposition

worse comes to worst I understand everything myself.

It looks the other way.

I, too, find it abstract as if to reconcile the beautiful world with thinking, so, something special, like money, has already happened in the beautiful world.

We make an inward account of the matter, following the outward show, a violent wheel draped in roses between sentiment and cynicism.

The whole party has new clothes.

See what time is, a good word encounters the difference.

That is abstract in good society.

A pact with the devil! The first reaction to my education.

Seven every distinct
from without in of
a the an any
comb combining take response

Spin is taken is distinct from spun.

Hence we can mean something if shifting from intend to and inexhaustible, self-generating.

Learning leads us to our deepest feelings.

We can mean that the deepest feelings are learned.

from with doubly:
with with the height of doubly:
the vertical is rolled with:

                doubt
the vertical
      roll   double   with double
shifting

      double the clarity in the thought lined

1977–1979

A life like this and must be sent as another pleasure.
Learning indulges itself with greed as before it can be brought to an end.
    For impulse generates.
    With cares.

       .   .   ..
       :   :   :

       privilege to be the work
       absurd romantic rest a noise
       the original theory submits to

all like but a
of again and in
is the of a in
or it in all a
like but a a a

    A brutal wresting.
    The result of a privileged childhood?
    Again: absurdly romantic, and in efforts not to be bourgeois.
    Writing is the work of thought—a theoretical original.

    A deliberate work, timed in good, or it thinks in iron.
    Sometimes all like events are childhood.
    Submissive and sentimental, but a brutal wresting.

       .   ,   ,   , . ⁻   .

    The whole originated in joyous association of my special form plays.

       ib   it
       im   od
       ss   ta
       ho   at

The Proposition

                    or

around or the least
motion, half alas,
that they meet, past
this only kept
history, written
against forgetting
that other memory

                Small part of all the learning innocent, and the meetings are as it is constantly reused.
                In the same movement the present is first sent for stuff tossed. As it does so, it is its own doing.
                It attempts while failing no omissions.
                Remember again that one imagines the years containing all that memory is an echo to be completely conscious. Much more than a stamping echo.
                For the sake of knowledge, immense, better, irrevocable.
                Studying the situation cigarettes. Seven-thirty. Respect. Problem.
                Half, alas.
                It is sent, we mean one look constantly reused, as if from a window prison, for a life in entrance capable of horizontal events lord vertical.
                The realities are really in that respect vigorous, problematic figures of antiquity and now.

the restless language
for knowing, it is
partial; the extension
of time is sent history
and the real present

                It is this time almost quietly no pace is out that leaving out is forgetting.
                Thinking is about following the dictates of a structure calls forth this extension the deep emotions of including hope, elation, doubt, despair, and uncertain but restless.

1977-1979

        Fists. Ransom. Damnation. Conscious of the
extreme is consciously believing which doubles
doubt, more a matter of perception, an unlevel
harmony. We do only a small part of all the
impatient meetings.
     With persons in it, generation.

the lines as first a

        The combing of the words creates the line a
thoughtful year.

            leg   his   ought
    The   years
               stamp

                   of form a the   conditions, a
or comment

    the   are general and   first but form

is seven every distinct from

    tend

pin   tin

The stamp of form is the second restatement

    (of the spin taken distinctly)

up are general the full stamp legibly from this year

        A full ocean and the seven thoughts suddenly
respond yet always extend through the years.
     The possible thoughts or the full years always
extend but legibly return in an ocean.

       extend the leg over thoughts is a seventh speculation
       or stamp of comment is flat and impossible

The Proposition

        The thought is suddenly general and the seven years are distinct.

ending our way into the oceans
topping the   best of waters that rise per
pendicular fuss with   any of them
                of what rest tips
went   There is the misunderstanding that defines us.

    Language is impatient, restless, partial,
characteristic of the curious greed of its users
    of which it also boasts against philosophy and the
subsequence
    of this partiality or defective change, or charge
    harsh and it doesn't please, first, solo, proof
    of the actual spatial come about it matters
    one cannot stop with any of them

    An unhesitating appropriation

    The inspiration of the incomplete

                    ans
                    ers
                    any
                    t r
                        and
                        rest
                  us

                      aga
                      fect
                      ase
                      me
                        o
                incomplete

    We depend on memory in order to read

1977-1979

The words are the shore between two natures. We make them that they meet. The share we have not even begun to examine is the ransom and damnation.

A fist is pulled open to the top part of it.

Discouragement, as if from a miserable window, clutching at the place is at this time a structure, under stress.

The sun is not kept out, but shines on the extension of a problem, library, year is set in motion, went constantly between what's known and what's to know.

Published in *Roof* 5 (winter 1978)
James Sherry, editor

1979–1981

Crooner

9.22 Soon over, the same moon moves. Hysterically present; lost without a trace. The chirping of dogs bank in a snow An oblong table fascinating me. I was leaving the library. Integrated parascript. A rhetorical yokel, a little page of the village. I had read a heavy Popeye. Newspaper stands slightly out of true. Returned to my zothecula. In Chinese singing perfect newspaperism. Bank robbed in a snow.

9.23 Sears at noon, open on Sunday. Streamlined cyclist ducks cars, bike flows with traffic. Prop shopping, but being too prompt, I eavesdropped on two big women. Every day one says I say my prayer. When I get too old to wait on myself, then Lord dismiss me. Baby powder. Crowds crockery. Money tomorrow turns to money powder, while we crimp, corrugate. Coin slots. I move red jack to black queen. Watching roller skaters with silent bearing. Then with Sunday paper eye the street.

9.24 Walk board road. Therefore the sky must be full of water. Amiable laundry. In chapters with the basket I am every morning its laundress. By afternoon flies. August spies. Spooks vamoose, those often showy flowers. Mean collie when saying dog. Thus make use of paranoia—yes, even negatively speaking. Definite thus, indefinite us. Sweater to the mountains. Rain road trail.

9.25 Evening. One more day less. This "elaboration now proclaimed and now disguised." Bare sole of shoe. The surface the city, a squaring sense of place. Sky blue tablecloth on picnic ground with title divined: Man of Agrarian Machine. A

The Proposition

complex of rooftops, perhaps a 'woman' of it. Every artist needs an Alice. Read writing over radio. The past was a thing of the author. Prose project. True (Greenwich) red in roses.

10.2 A space in the garden. Ace up. To my left, under my arm, the arm of my chair. Hand things—school sweets—an almond in the rough. "A calculation as an ornament is also formalism." Bedecked with live lilies, one takes great liberties, in fact an army. Finds its shabby replacement. The buildings are taped to the city. Remove troops I suppose—the dog's name. Pencil over window pane. Paved color. The flower itself is to me even busy.

10.10 They photographed all day, then developed all night. In translation, chirping old ballads over strings of phones. Picabia. Jazz media. We used to count to one with one eye in good measure. Drops trickling up speed. A projection of oneself however from emerging. The breeze plays fair on water, fans the deck. Sunshine and penumbra. Perhaps inevitably interior. Audacity turned inward, the city stature visual cover. Life styles store house.

10.11 I see starlight in the sky on the wall. "By the wind impaled." Tar star below. Flat arts. Negative echo of oblong tale. It describes no floor-wall combinations. Simple addition in two rows of five, street and sky. Artificial ice, vanilla glass. Cottage curds. The curtains cross safely at the window. Over border, for deeds to come, "the din is the applause of objects." From National Public Radio I get some of the Chinese chant: sing hang Sam ring.

10.12 Rain on the laundry dries as it begins to clear. Sound travels—descending by the stairsteps to the ramp up. Mesh through, neat. Rayon. In the neighborhood houses all colors closeted. Walls stucco. Zip unknown. These strange material buckaroos blink. Near neighbors pop music. This morning went to take a walk. In the yard, in a book, in a chair, in the afternoon—with the leisure to be anarchists. What it, began to·rain.

1979–1981

10.13   I read for the trees, acutely, in camera. Latex palace. Book but not specs. There is where intellectual sin starts. Head lines, picture points. The little word "one" is the general but intimate pronoun. A deep "I." Screen windows grid my view. I grin out as shoppers pass from nothing to nothing more. Taping penlight to pillow, kilomiles folding under pad. Shuttered in camber. Bound by the pane.

10.16   Stunt riders ring binder. Letter head. Work in chapters cans the chatter. Encyclopedic can held around such a fire. Touch hot pot, walk out into traffic. To the left and right, houses. Trees inter view. Song borne on on leg of lyric. Lyric burden. Eric Partridge. Finch against sky of a digital blue. Not colored through.

10.20   Boats in pond park. Duck and rock in mud. Pure rubber. Yellow screen. I want to return now to that chapter of our lives. A back log. We can't. From a full sentence, digits whittled off. Scoop of rubric. Bumbles over flower. I put it down on the spot. "A desk into whose drawers I proceeded to pour sand."

10.22   Sun spot. Three-score thorn. Footsteps heard on the stair herald a hand on the door. Tree-lorn—a solid citizen, or a housebreaker. Lower, as the weather when the rain's allowed to fall. Broadcast misnomer. Even Duke Ellington used to get mad. The unbroken brunt of a solid. We drive back from the city. The children are sincerely silly. Stretch to the finish line. Silence even more abstract.

Documentary

A road. Profuse. The documentary. Overall. A market day. Milk melts.

Enter a shop selling food baskets, a proper display of details. Tuna stinks. Seven doubles four. Notice the dog's soulful upward gaze.

Daredevil helicoptrist. The white tin spins without wheels. Realism is the emotional machine become anonymous.

The rose does not become an apple beyond the doorway of the fire station.

The gasoline is pumped into the cars from the joggers' treadmill, and the money moves faster. Runners spend.

Horses untended break out of their corrals and rush pasturing into the fields of wheat. They are isolated within this comfort.

Everyday objects are heroic, such as the clothespin, dishrag, toothbrush. Travel forward toward the pile of books. A second kick sends it forward. And for that matter in letter, too. Such a literate crowd! And in all other instances where certain words have to drive it home.

Tempo starts. As hopping; unfolded movement. All dissimilar events. Historical stately clusters period.

They have not necessarily rejected the thirteenth note and apple, nor a reasonable memory of the workplace. The swerving of the

The Proposition

hour of midnight. Let the dark of the leaves all at once fall into a complex of allusions.

Old familiar places haunt them more than the new ones. It looks like a lot in the gray of greenery in photographs. The porch is around two sides of the house before it finishes. Such gaps and fragmentation as a reader might be moved to fill.

Anyone can have his horse fall over as it walks along. Napoleon always said has he got luck.

They step back in the alley-way and true the pile upright.

The radio moves the still night on. They drive into the city, in a series of highlights punctuated by stoplights. Draw electricity.

Bike spokes, books. A box of lug nuts, bowl of pods, some cups; all consequences. What does it not mean. Until we no longer have to oscillate, with the countermovement that replaces infinity, searching here, searching there, trying to get away, returning home. A primary and intentional concern in writing is such movement as that.

They shift from an image expected in practical speech. Captains only 4 steps backward. Tires lift the back lights. Indistinguishes trash in garbage. Lines up when they meet are not quite right, not similar.

They are down on their knees scrubbing at the floor, then up on the ladder scrubbing windows. Askew meet parallels. Rush seeping out on the wet blue-orange street.

Shadow, door, shoreway. Weights of work. A person amplifies what's said, and the quality wakes them up. The lights brighten if the room cools.

Liquid has power always over solid. Thinking makes it between. It is to move once more. A solitary fishing boat is making for . . .

1979–1981

In a direct line from New York, sticking to history (from the real to the more real) and the observed moved world. Stark telephone, with ring, wire, pole.

A billboard for the moment at a roadside is fixed into the world of its artificial greens. But everything is different. Always.

It has acquired the status of an event in its own right. A halting pen with which to employ it. Before, they spaded in a garden.

No where, no place. But nothing, too, much more than hits this. Static breaks the source of silence. Wet tin green-red rings.

In short, be prehistoric boys and girls. Scratch in space.

Published in *Soup* (1980)
Steve Abbott, editor

Seven

Rains in the sun. Spring's winter and go shopping. Bullfrogs squat. Why it is! What it is! We can mince around the sprinklers or we can go through.

We unite the moving particles in this form. The argument, transformed. Household hollycocks. Heroic porch guard.

Outside inside—if we insist on Monet.

Enough to go out on a wet night in the cold. The crooked man with crooked stick walks his crooked mile.

One street. Another. The address is at the exit. The drone of the traffic is interrupted by a silent night.

In this form the roads mince, until the sun burns. The little purple flowers warm. One, the finch, is flying, sign and implication, overlooks full shops. In a backyard, many children, both girls and boys, in many countries, play with mud. They are building forts and towns connected by roads merely two fingers wide.

The sheriff, a kick, one foot, the hero. Let's stop here. Good-bye to our past.

Published in *Soup* (1980)
Steve Abbott, editor

Short Arbiter
(for Henry Kaiser)

The clouds flat, the door white.

In check the bedsprings walk.

Light passes around an opaque edge.

A flight of steps ascends a spur of mountains.

The hideous access mars the lure of the sea.

The deliberate spelling is a thin disguise.

All smiles, then a tram.

A camera for another.

I would like to walk around the streets looking like a trumpet.

The rim a receding diagonal, the horizon its restless edge.

I look at landscapes under lamplight in color plates on slick paper without texture, perfectly flat, tipped into the volume.

This is almost comical in its gravity.

Through the grass and under a plank at the flat lower half of the pasture runs the creek.

Pitched materials are picked from a continuum.

The Proposition

Cube hedges surround the outdoor stove.

One end of the tug of war is seized.

Love perpetuates one's interest in an old-fashioned medium, the printed page.

This is translated tit for tat.

The distance isn't silent.

Kansas seems exotic.

Such is a necessity of castle-building.

The flowers are studied with numerative scruple.

The last sound I make is left hanging.

Why "pay" attention.

Pilot silences.

This is compounded of desire to save the world and of personal ambition.

These pages flame with amorous adventures, flanked by blanks moved back.

We cannot close our ears; we have no ear lids.

Society has no fringe.

The sea does what it likes, and what it likes is destruction.

These are outbursts of idealism.

Minute discriminations release poetic rather than cerebral effects.

I take this stake in my left hand and the hammer in my right.

1979–1981

The eyes are a medium for what one knows but sensitive to only a tiny part of it.

The speaker reaches the hearts of her hearers.

Their hearts give stone the pulsation sought by enthusiasts.

There is an old taboo against an artist's attempt to make a living thing.

I rifle the apple tree.

The sounds fall into parts.

Mass exactness.

I am realistic; others are sensational.

I am not emotionless but these emotions are, in the main, intellectual.

Shells in the backyard suggest that the building rests in an ancient sea bed.

Cynicism and aloofness, far from being a pose, spring from nature.

This punctuation has no word.

A coincidence occupies the same place, changing dirt to gold.

Hoisted after heavy rain.

Everything's cool; solace forests.

Inevitability is no barrier to tension.

The sunlight shining from the right virtually blocks out the view.

For the moment, a particular static, an interplay, at the surface of the window pane, allows charge but prevents exchange.

Remarkable scratches, nicks, notches, intervene.

Severed Page

Raise of day at severed page. Some green grass grows under a weekend visit. "Sitting in diamonds among the midges." Washington rallies his troops at Monmouth. A bright light on the breast of a brown horse. Others pass. No fact is less "anymore than our senses show us the present." Children climbing on a sculpture slide down, spun around. Stable. A consoling declaration. A war of minds. Stately trees, ochre building *en face*, the street clenched. Paranoia, but with inventions hoarded. The boards of a hut held up by pins. Who can win such a war, and, if winning, would. A useful thorn in the side would silence the scene. Spare parts. This alp crossed by an elephant. Objects on the surfaces restore the horizon. On the left a cool landscape of mountains, clouds. Evergreens are casting blue shadows over the smoke of battle. "I would like to walk around the streets looking like a trumpet." Through doors. Leaves blowing down leaving the tree. Clouds swirl and it is unclear, a fiction in the description. This is an illusion. The house in a way of the view. At a stagnant pond a man and a dog drink, the dog with its mouth to the water, the man dipping his hat into it. "The first had the fussiness of attempted accuracy, the second more differences." Sentences collapse together. An echo in every work. When dawn goes down, day comes up. Stacked on a curve. Charles Lee is in the act of turning back.

1979–1981

I brown study
no stars

take any such point and join it with a bundle
who invents paper

this rooms reenter
this stage must be allowed to dry

three stories, myself among them
jogged for the tuner

this house had never any where-we-live
as hitherto, if you wish; I do

famous record
under roof over sky

reruns the curve
what time it is phrase through it

shoes flower
of more or less rubber

lap in the air glass acts
sky doesn't spoon

the fits
a piece of drinking hay, in juice soda

the stars park poses apart
lowers the eyes

one of the woof
if you cry

you-all smirk
in no star system

Published in *This* 10 (winter 1979–80)
Barrett Watten, editor

Felicity

1.

Felicity from or by whom fanned up a minimum in the right mind emerging. Thatch setting hangs field day. Wide erasures open hills. Black mutt on seeing irritability, one of humor. From the balcony we lean over the rotaries and their birds. Redundant quiet nearer the norm to be visible figures exterior. Wings orderly incline. In daylight emerging authenticity separates the trees. The thick edge of the wedge follows. The clouds flat, the foreground wide, approaches of the glass bottom boat nodding in the air. A canary needs a little light and a wall. States of patience is banal. Shows a cloud. A uniform light for a minute all the way around on the horizon line they hang. Birds sit on the slope of a neighboring roof where I've never observed them before. A thin disguise is subject to their circumspection. Eventual tug full of birds. Additional details sought by enthusiasts in a superlative degree compare setting only on green things. The terrestrial investigator waters the garden. Jumbo windows nodding in the air. Idle minds are subject to acute dark. A wedge of flying in winter-time. Wide exile then all smiles isn't pitched and virtually in realistic color replicates. Blank length of incidence idle minds the field day.

2.

Erasures a rosy reported nuance nodding in the air. The eye level casual in case the rhapsody is splay. Spare cemeteries duplicate silence enjoining ridiculous domus display: "the famous close up of a doggy look." Someone called Pierre Toussaint injects his brain with a euphoria-inducing drug which enables him to regard himself in the mirror. The foreground chosen at random duplicates Donna.

1979–1981

The yield of the forenoon fins a flight of steps. On a pedestrian trip of observation no barrier trips to Mars. Snorkelers chase the Moorish idols that while performing it did not swerve in the slightest form from a square front to the group. Proves on this little sailing trip heavy rains up to the spurious reef shows up in shallow distortion. For Rodney has suffered a head wound while discovering an immense metal city buried under his farm. Such scenic accidents separate trees. Such prosaic explanations as a flight of birds near the surface or actually swimming on·the surface may account for the spur of mountains. Scratches, notches illuminated and animated. A changing sign in a uniform light. Telescopic pincers wave of the forenoon on its square front.

3.

Duly light lulls foliage etched in bestiary nouns. And loving to watch unseen, all smiles, inducing skepticism. Knocks on glass. The llama rocks. The roots of the tree send feeders into the mulch. Denizens preoccupy the foreground fix on its hippic figures. Ours a fine climate templates nothing in the air. The changeling returns in a switch proves the show farm may amount to silver spurs. Anywhere flowers grown brown can rebloom edgewise. Pick of scheming niches a pigeon-house columbines entwine. It seems you never can forget your railroad-poetry, Aramasia remarks, reading the food buttons. Water greedily sleek at ordinary speeds forensic. Which owns up a cow pony nudged out following the wedge of canal notches. First westerns sung combines with hubbub, its floral grill. Camels successfully introduced into Texas follow a number of new words describing the patience and bravery of camels. Connected harangues got in edgewise, the Ultra.

4.

Mud on a calm day emitting a green. The electric ray out of the indigo sea. Is jumbo, inducing the minimum. A half dozen creatures spared by rust waters the garden. The buzz of a calabash naturally thatch. Nourished by dust in a black mutt's ear. Multicelled abundance circumscribes form. Setting at celsius redundant norms. Joe wins the heart of Donna whom he marries in spite of her horns. Euphoria yields the spurious reef to a natural trickery they light up. Remind dreams motivating the vigilance of

The Proposition

field trips. Banal clouds the color and texture of thimbles its metal shines. The plot on its own properly occupies the rotary. Radio turned at a carousel pace what's superstition to Huck Finn. Figures exterior mannerisms, for whom fanning: Pierre. The thick wedge of additional details about to fly as the stone hangs. We lean over the borderline. Idle minds at eye level amount. The changing signs in a uniform light combine. It is twice as interesting if while painting a nest one dreams of a cottage.

Published in *Some Other Magazine*, no. 5 (summer 1981)

The Theme

I wear a red shirt, the sky is blue, and I think magenta, green, a patted dam, a puddle, mud, sitting for my contemplation.

I begin in place with the character of a line defined, but dreamed last night of a fountain pen, or less the pen than the forms it made, broad, even blunt, which did not 'read'; that is, I don't recall that they 'said' anything for the moment (the impression won't survive).

There is a lucky accident, a valid tackle, a fling united. It was forgettable, now it is trapped, exists, exact, an accent in the artist's favor. It could not fail of certainty, a factory, in the world of utensils, junk totems on the walls. At a mortal distance from the eye, held in the air, to the light, an odd superior, given shape, an elevation, sunrise, air folded in stone, sides scurrying up, the door distinct, the upsurge composed, a small hill forever turning. Urbino is pink, pink encloses Urbino.

Pronounced an expert, I hear a dimestore violin, an illusion, with all its omissions forestalled.

A primitive curiosity compels us to finish. I took up my book eagerly, glanced up reluctantly, realizing scarcely any mention of what I might do one day.

The water dries, is lighter and more portable. Decay escapes, a detail remains, comes clear, after a curious delay, a bloom reviewed, allowing all that was separate to remain separate.

The Proposition

I make a perfect scale of reduction, basalt. Erosion clears a hold and the landscape can't break away, translated into bits of steel, bits of choice, a battle face, a history, one's fill of realism.

I reflect a voluntary account, premeditate, a summer picnic, the term of a diary, realistic arrangements of historical forms, a whole other version, in rowdy color, lined up by the creek, eating. Frogs are changelings. Brown, green, naturalisms from the bottom rise to power; what might be, what might have been.

Published in *QU* 3 (1980)
Carla Harryman, editor

The Supplement

Nothing prior to color. They sing funny little numbers all praising the numerous pleasures. The fog lifts a late sunrise. There are floral twigs in position on it. A paper hat afloat on a cone of water. Four seasons circling one square year. The mud cracks and the tadpoles turn in the nick of time to frogs. Technical infill, simple belief arithmetic. My sister sucks her catsup up the straw, which the waitress crumples up, clearing off, and the catsup shoots out. I was hiding high up in a tree, waiting for Indians to appear and kill the bear. I read transition fiction, saw blue in a golden memory. A string of noble phrases, rashes. It is a work of architecture. Or a hand of canasta, the game at which Gram cheats. I am urged out (rummaging) into the sunshine, and the depths (celestial) increase (of blue) above. A fen in the landscape, the copse eclipsed. They are sitting in the car in careful order, man in front at wheel, wife beside as navigator. They think I am fated for the life of a painter because I link thinking to colors. Any noise, radio, or conversation in the same room circles as if detachable. I live in a block, squaring up. Overstep. I shop to Muzak with its chewy beat between things of the same kind that are separated only by time. Race down as soon as it opens and get a parking place, married, a book, a bargain, a cold, the joke, warm, home early. In the car I get the window. Drain ruins the snow. I watch from the elevated loges of the theater. A tenant in this situation lives like a bird in a tree. The baby is scrubbed everywhere, an apple. Bitten by an ant. They are not interested in man's emotional upheavals but in his eccentric movements in space. The Swahili for football, mañana cannon, eskimo pies. All families make a concerted instamatic effort. Hesperian (palm) blue, hyperborean blue, Euclidean blue. The neighbors to the left complain about the volume of music. I can only offer the apologies I have committed. Or can't we think

The Proposition

there's existence in ideas too. I don't discover the world—the words do that, the three-quarters view revealing something of the sitter's character.

The signature a tour de force in picket. Occasionally when the wind has fallen, the poplars continue to lean at cross-purposes. They are against the blue. I stand at the stop reading posted information: College, University—Seven-11, exact change. For 60 billion a metro for missiles is matched against what. An "initial shock," my own. I spread my fist, I resort to my fingers. One moves from the inside, a likeness featured in a window frame, appreciating all/any landscapes, architectures. Red tile styles, rank smell of lively slime, red neck avocets in the distance, bubbles buried in the mud—this was her childhood estuary. One forgets and regrets it. Dissimilar elements grow closer—I diphthong. Horde. Window washers appear in appropriate glass slots. Open improviser's fresh ayre. I hear the creak down river of a distant train on the tracks, carrying lumber in the sun down valley. In suspense a plumb line. A form with fat in it: twelve tone twelve bar. We are likely to find ourselves pondering suchness as the essence of bourgeois memorabilia. We go back to the beach, past the signs of a tide at Devil's Slide, mud on the Grapevine, hailstones on Weedpatch. Liquid paper. "Tear stone" or "eat broom"—small recombinations of parts of the environment. And at the corners, a puddle of snow, melting, blowing hot and cold. I quadrille by and by. In circular breathing, take no breath (break). Detail detail, echo echo, overtly real. The perpetual annual show. On the rock walks at the Rose Garden with other walkers I look lopsided, hobble, come to see the flowers. Struck with my vision all would do likewise. Lovers cannot be expected to read minds. I see my own short-term short-sightedness, extend lines from a single point, identify trends from one particular, always happy, forever despairing. The window is like a magnet. I felt that I had accomplished the exit because I read the sign. Psalm Reader, in Salinas. In the wind a trespassing of cows under the clouds settles in the vacant lot. Postcards of scrapbook semi-views pasted up. I make a picaresque attempt to return. Pilfer near the rural in the word nature. Balancing a low horizon, vanishing vernal day.

Published in *Periodics* 7/8 (winter 1981)

1981–1982

1981–1982

    The erosion of rocks blooms. The world
       that's for you thanks (you) in actuality actuality.
    Large broad marks without interruption.
       Things as they fall in the hotel reduce
    the view. This is the world you
    all add up to, the miniature terms of detail.

    Sugar, less coffee, a clean towel, the archive.
       All add up to from the minute after after all.
     The theater is less exciting. The shore worn
    potable. The erosion of rocks less salt.
       A carnival for posterity is a machine
    in its early stages. A clean towel
     pulled out. The theater suggests a house
     a machine. I am irritated by this
    contradictious optimism. The world pretends
     to get a fair distance on unshod horses.
    The theater shares the optimism of the carnival.

     A conservative year is a suggestion. The mechanical
    use of photos yours. Using nails
       reduces the view. Things fall some of the way
     out into the street a new scene. A grid
    worn by water from one place to another. The erosion
    of rocks washed away. The theater of holes dug for trees.

Published in *Sun & Moon* 11 (spring 1981)
Douglas Messerli, editor

The Military

The military is ironic but its damage
would be of little use. The second
invasion is entirely satirical.
A glare comes off a guard—
Good ... Bad ... Sacrifice ... Life ...

argues society, hovering without reserve.
They say in the bookshops, "Give me some books
with blue covers." So many people
have arrogantly thought that if *they* prayed
for a better world it would occur.

Any level spot could be the first solid ground
   under one's feet. Scan mechanically,
   they look blindly beyond. Green,
at the close of a colorful countryside.
The house collapses sunlight, found
   its fortune in the ground here.
Sunset at sea level, fact beyond invention,
brought down to the water, better searched
         than sunk.

The Proposition

    The inanimate are rocks, desks, bubble,
        mineral, ramps. It is the concrete being
    that reasons. The baseboard weighing
    its wall span. The clouds never form regiments
        and don't match. The gap in my education
    needn't be filled. Stubbornness is provocative.

    The pessimist suppresses a generous anger. A trace
        linked to a fence of forgetting. Lying awake
    may serve the purpose that dreams do. In the dark
    opaque disposal of the missing past. Canned laughter
        is white noise. Comparable repositories of freight dust
    into the shadows. Anger is the animate of stubbornness.

Published in *Sulfur* 5 (1982)
Clayton Eshleman, editor

Rain on the macadam quaver ticks.
The lay of the land is armed
with its pattern of occupancy.
Landscape depends on sequel, is romantic ground
in a context of necessity. Polish tinfoil
with pennies and make silver.
Windows upon close inspection swing, medaled
with the setting. Highlights work
back and forth, relocate to swap greenery.
The finished man is horizontal, a cliché.
The watch hand is a pointer
through thick lenses on a setting.
Statues have status in the park.
All one can do is go around them, directed
by the curve. Return to lengthwise.

Published in *Sulfur* 5 (1982)
Clayton Eshleman, editor

The Proposition

    Under the radio roof, a mere wisp
from witchcraft to medicine. An expectant melismata
    squandered. The landscape flushes green.
    How many plants compound clarity.
Low windows run the simile; only the word brick
in the description. The limits of the sky in scattered light
    refer to clouds reflecting in a creek.
    The remote present (as of now)
    in a compass wall, glass. The rigid side
    of a hedge. The proven mobile home
takes to a country surface. The bullseye darts aside.
    The advantage of a double horizon
is a temporary description, a split or repercussion
    in the fitting home as of a boat at sea
which floats by drawing nearer. Only the word brick
is accurate in the dramatic banter, in that timidity
    of intellect where everything is relevant.

Published in *Sulfur* 5 (1982)
Clayton Eshleman, editor

1981–1982

The blue-green northeast lake props its aureole.
    False front of hill approach
mounted horizontal outcrop. Yodeling vanquishes care.

    A plant sports forth in bud
above the harbor salvo. Substantiating facts leap
       thin taste in the tin of shade.

    Lumbers buried in weeds.
Overhead countryside built in the western vagueness.
    The bird's flight is a concave arc.

    A flying running band of clouds
dents the line along the horizon's imperfect meeting space,
       prospects of unpopulated chances.

A gravely regular scratch in a nutshell,
    these colors on the inside. A daydream
in the miniature exemplified by the weed.

Published in *Sulfur* 5 (1982)
Clayton Eshleman, editor

The Proposition

    It rained all afternoon. Plots abut
        the milk of glass leveled along an oblong
    green. The glare throws shadows in odd directions,
          shakes the distinctive shimmer. The sky removes
      absolutism with changing moods, of wool and gold.

    A dirty secondary heap has for its object
        mutual assistance. A link with the staggering store
        is forged. The minimally knotted walls prop
the description. Specifically the general type
      is pierced by its phenomena.

    Dry days are bright in the mornings
        in ganglions. The instant blinks, the eye
    not merely flat. They take unnecessary steps to cover
      the traces they haven't left. One sees
      how they come out.

    The dogged sunniness shines. The light scatters
        shadows it could cloud over the corner.
    A mall, slim, abuts the public sidewalks.
    Vacant lots, money aprons, prostrate trunks portion
        off the shore.

Published in *Sulfur* 5 (1982)
Clayton Eshleman, editor

Mental watchdog, the brainstorm's over,
a lodestar's in the mist.
New uses for a fluid masonry.
Glass mouthless, an honest stone,
all musical strings running mirrors.
Rooms at all odds of identity
are within them over a giant tempo
running torpor in subsidence time.

Life for its advantages almost rises
visible feet. Raised shadow without clouds
of mass fecundity. Those that shine back
fling relatively local blanks
between the hand and sidewalk.
The eyes as the bird flies averted
face to the regular article
there though the thought turns them.

Published in *Sulfur* 5 (1982)
Clayton Eshleman, editor

The Proposition

The tidal throughway from a distance
dispersing everything sloppy, anything
resembling an excessive spell. All that's left
is lambent, like lakes. One misses
the remarkable detail of continuity.
Light devours the visible world.
A slack windsock, sole identified sequence.

The garrulous landscape is stoked
and synoptic; the synonym list
is doggedly on plot, gleaming
in the sunlight, husbanded with enchantment.
The glass on the way down flowers. I did
or am doing in common speech fully informed,
unafraid of repetition in the same person.

Published in *Sulfur* 5 (1982)
Clayton Eshleman, editor

1981–1982

pandemonium hews
no clouds

wakefulness
is active

one is a statistic
an ideal of exhaustiveness

it meets this
precise redundant limbo

stars of keyholes
laud the rain cloud

shapes sloshing
off an awkward clay

a sea that only scatters
in a halfbox

the gloss of observation
in the dark

the sounds are in the ears
a prima ragged brio

mute water crashes rise
in a cloud

Published in *Sulfur* 5 (1982)
Clayton Eshleman, editor

The Proposition

    Shade cows stand

    See reflection
    fill up this reason

    Latin faces at the asphalt delta

    Glances mowing over
    flowers into flooring

    Rolled boredom accumulates room

    Thus music struck
    if memory squeaks

    Flowering is genial

    Turf and competence
    pierce shallows

Published in *Popular Poetix* 2 (spring 1982)

Arms

The flush brunt levels reason
   Unlimited armed wings
Limbs dangle from the stick
pathetic in the reduction to a word of view
   Camouflage blooms
with resemblance not coincidence
The North Pole is hot
   A gingko fans
pressing shadows fit to nickname
   Nonetheless less moon
   a dented proto-light
from the point of view of view
brought over with binoculars

The temperate is like cardboard
relocates land messages, geysers
   or ore in masonry
Copies dote, shadow's shot
a color made shape in a blood frost
   'it deteriorates into song'
The knot not coincidence
   An angle beating reason
   lodged in the medium

The floor is going faster than a fan
Several marches bathed in sunlight
   of some inspired staples
planted in segments of a diameter
   Aside lie palisades
a bar of sand and island petals in the rain

The Proposition

    Anatomy hobbled between flowers
sweeps away the weeds burning downwind
Being enthusiastic in advance we feed
    from the postponement
By repeating silence change
    Praise is balm
beaten into echoes from particulars

    Slantwise wanderlust
with the 'prudence' of a nail
planted in its 'real name' an audit
    venting flats
Protected songbirds recoil to the upper limit
Rose stumps dovetailed with blue twigs
    leave leaves on lateral
the silent weather prodded through
    citizens in their·geometry
    moving house

    A dome of dumb air
    no mortars roll
    'loosen the attention'
The escape tendency excludes usefulness
Wheels foot fields, forge street plans
    rhyming mates
swarm until comfortable
Perennials confide flowers
in 'ungoverned stations'
    Air rifles condition
    A bodily post
clutching an elated chronology

    Subject figures 'downcast, unwilling
        to be disturbed'
Equipoise describes the mellow warrior
    The day moreover over
the lives of shapes that ricochet
    the normal honors

1981–1982

The music makes one maudlin—or jumpy
  Big stumbling cushions
  from its magnetic stock
in range of impetuous pity

Open handed traces dead pan
  lodged a tested forecast
Experience goes unrepeated
  so life is lost
  Memory merely copies
a reserve 'ensemble of possible states'
kept to oneself who is 'soft'
The will will bend nerves
  grieve over evil
  The sky builds up
A skirmish bivouacs its field tension
Furious rust thus intrinsically times
  'impress the world'

Published in *This* 12 (fall 1982)
Barrett Watten, editor

Two Cities

I'd like to begin in Boston in a candy store at a tiny fountain reading through the cash register. "First come, first served" is an impersonal remark. That is the one consolation that is going to make me sleep nights.

I am disguised as a wrangler. My bandana is my only luxury and it is tied around my neck like a milestone.

It is morning and out of the dark the drifting light forces the window. In a few minutes I'll have a good view. It is a curious thing, that height of many feet. No doors shut out my capacity to face the open universe, and I am not yet caught by the hint of movement in the middle of the deserted street.

The all night vigil has come and gone. It had the caressing aura of a séance, a half-world murder, reborn slowly. Owl hoots were brought to a halt.

A taxi is shining under the nose of an old man. I'll pay in a year, he's heard to say, but that depends on how we define every penny. If you're playing with the rent, you'll lose. If there are two of you, one chooses solitude.

There was a time when I studied my elbows by crossing my arms and walking. It appears that the material of my life is inexhaustible. The dials are for volume.

It is a slow Monday and warm in San Francisco, where I am checking out Market Street, mixing a little of this business with

sunshine. The members of the Salvation Army band smile with
radiant melancholy and wave their tambourines. I hum back.

I never learned enough details, either to sing or to fell timber.
Hammering my toes to make them softer, I have done all my
dancing for a better grab on the floor. The gateway to the skies
reaches over the full acre.

My one thought is to overtake the fatal hour. When I give the word
we'll ride out at 70 onto 580 into the Central Valley as the day's
first sunlight shines past us into the whitecaps of the bay. The
result of our drive will be two parallel lines. Listen for the tone. I
hate station wagons, and I dislike games, having no inclination to
win and pitying the foolish loser with an extreme sentimentality.

The two halves of my first dollar have gone into the mainstream.
Every ten cents pays for twenty-five hours of singing cowboys,
gaining on mighty strides. If they could, they would gather up their
pink slips and birth certificates and head straight for the mid-
Western woods. From there they would do absolutely nothing
more than miss seafood.

In the meantime, back in Boston, that theater of the mind, I get
some sleep. A lot of good isn't much. These are not Milton's
efforts to justify God's difficult providence.

I myself can read the inside story of a locked book: a 600 page
biography with a cluttered desk on the wall and the windows
covered with dusty, hence palpable, light. I connect the source with
the stream, though it waves back and forth, sounding off before
day and night.

No questions, no signature. What has the phonograph done for the
ear. I have assumed that Malibu is the namesake of an animal, a
mammal or a fish, as in caribou and halibut.

I change from my disguise to my mask. Looks are deceiving,
which is my business. The red brick throws off all pursuers.

The Proposition

Being of methodical temperament, I have thoroughly searched Value Village, thumping the green slopes. I have kept a grim record of the dramas I have witnessed during this period. There is no more than 10 % art in radios.

You know Sutter's Gold
(for Barrett Watten)

Do I have the tree of my uncle's garden. The brown ground has faded to purple. Aerial landscapes are much ahead and who could believe these impossible things before breakfast.
    We looked out at the early landscape color. The shutter was hinged back a few feet outside the window, in an open position, its shadow either pushing or hanging over the yellow poppies and natural blue clumps of rosemary. We look forth across the window instead. Close to the window there is a smell of mildew, roses, and tomatoes. The room is reassuring, in out of the weather. This is not the first time I've been glad of the sun flagging on the wooden floor.
    But the western journey was to be one of families, and so to come closer home. The neighbor's mother had about her the smell of wet wool, and so we found her European; her purple satin had faded to brown. She was tired of the life and thought she would quit soon and go back to her own country. In her learned way she says the main charm is that we go back to nature, where we belong.
    Whatever it might be, there appeared to be now some hope of finding it. One bit of matter in quite a bit of range.
    The true America lay in that endless intervening. The fat cow grazes upright. Buttered crackers, Sutter's gold. That's the charm and it would be a great life were it not for the nights and the lonely cabin with only one's thoughts for company. At the door I let the dog out and he runs around the fir trees barking at the squirrels; he barrels quite naturally into the woods. It was quiet during my one visit to the church, into which we walked like a big train. So a drunkard and a talkative woman spread the news.

The Proposition

When he rode over to the mill in the morning to reconnoiter he spoke of his melancholy ride. The revolving sprinklers were watering the lawns, just hitting at the edge of the sidewalk, which gave off its smell of a better, rainy, day, and a deeper shade of gray. We went inside to see the yellow landscapes. The green was cast between the yellow of the imagined ground and the painter's painted skies or water. There the reader and I might go together, backwards on our path.

Some of these liked the exile and found a way to stay, but others fled with an unhappiness that gold could not console. They praised the sky, painted the land. Of course, we like the speed of transaction here, in the golden gloom. The roses are sensational in the repose at which we gaze.

Two weeks later I took up my pen. The grass is coming up, the hillsides are all green, and it looks like spring instead of fall. It moves out of one pocket into the other and back again. Confronted by those enormous blue billows one can go no further. Nobody knows what to do with the money, as it is not known where it came from. But it was bad to learn there was no place to stop on the way.

It seems a pity that when it is all worked out there will be nothing to stay for. I did some work last week that brought back old times. I don't mind them so much, but you never can tell where you'll be on the morrow. The brush was still wet from the rain yesterday and the water of the brook was not as clear and amber-colored as usual. Rose, named for her beauty, which was considerable, as was her spread and weight, is such a speculation.

How can one in this case continue a destruction when anyway there was nothing left now. It is time to be doing something. A simple problem—tramp around. Walk there, walking slowly. It happens you've got a good view, facing backgrounds. The rocks, rather black, lean over the creek. Pure, the water swerves, brown and green as usual. I am gratified, if it does, lagging on afterwards, mud falling off the clouds. It casts lots and proves gold, and that was an obvious thing to like to look at.

Sitting in the cabin door and looking out in the woods, one can't help noticing the different shades of green. I don't think I will fill them, neither will I start another one. No, but I have the rosebush of my cousin.

The Pit

The cold in this luminous season
stings. Sense data sinks.
Low rooves cover over restorative content
in an intimate world of form.
I'm witness to a monography, 'words standing
for words.' Dreams are false secrets.
Hyperbole acquires details. The range wavers.
The murderer I personify aims
through a yoke hole. The pale network
of the shack lost in gaps. Grassy growth
repeats close to the logic of flack.

The sea faces the sky, over one day's cover
in close proximity. Sense data rises,
uneven grass denies chronology.
Spotters at watching posts are set
among poppies. The synchronous runs out
of familiar faces. The myopic with a telescope
personifies a lost profile, hyperbole
with an emulous hitch, the dream
a reaction more likely than experience.

Province

The town is a whistler
turn on a rock
The water runs a working curve

A taste never rested
architecturally horizontal between tides
Puddles fill a fresh safety

Sunsets swarming
an igloo on the right day
Perhaps affinity is the 'maverick'

Posted flowers
to stakes of rain
I recede in a structure of feeling

derogatory and prolific
Fate strikes while one sleeps
encyclopedic syntax

Curricular luck
in an apparent withdrawal
(that which went without saying)

Birds and neighbors' radios
deftly with a board
refill the room

'reading meanings' my knees
then stare—the exchange

The Proposition

    fits reality neatly

    A random stone raps the shadow
    With one interest light corrected dreams
    Themes read as Greek

    the patience of a panorama
    The scale is closed
    The span has an instinct for ellipses

    subjunctive strangeness
    The scud casts doubt on status in addition
    fills unclouding

    file across scan
    A return on your identification
    threatens evolution

    skimping the subjective
    Ants are hysterical about social detail
    Canons of resemblance

    are in the solvent frame
    Every turnip strives to be a man
    proenforcement, prolific subtotals, flat gates

    professions of attention span
    The color has a bend in it
    The corrugate perceptions raise trajectories

    fascination nags

Exit

Patience is laid out on my paper
is floodlit. Everything's simile.
The cadence is detected, the cipher is broken, resolved
the sky bears the enjambments, heavy clouds
the measure of one with a number block
changes shade. The flow of thoughts—impossible!
with which we are so familiar. The river
its visuals are gainful and equably square
in an automatic writing. Self-consciousness
to reclaim imagination . . . to rise early
that is, logic exaggerates the visible
to oppose laziness. Unto itself, built of bricks
is a cumbersome monument on whom motion
is bent over, having sunk a fork into the ground.

Published in *This* 12 (fall 1982)
Barrett Watten, editor

Resistance

With better bacteria, 'man could live by tree alone.'
Themes or theses read as Greek.
Struck flowers rise.

The green fields are sharp
overdescriptions
they support like pencils. Learning accrues waysides.

As physics lists
a city of whistles registered.
And the rectangle down there on the floor. Ha ha.

'Spring it is spring why.'
Reasons are so numerous
—leaves the ore to grow—

subject to ridicule, naked but for socks
secured objectivity.
Great hoods are lasting buildings.

The admiration for appearances (paranoia)
prohibited scope.
I don't know what the punctuation is at the end.

Rhyme pinned to the sides
'my imperfections on my head.'
Getting it out of life

'prose was born yesterday.'
The frontage knocks
the potholes, colors filled with hay.

1981–1982

I'll add a brick. The electron
is almost anonymous. An egg (melodrama!)
weighs way more. 'Outreach' serving signals.

After the cast a rake draws points
at neighborish flanking. Returns, earshot of all sorts,
the psychological punctures. Or cynical bootstraps.

Hand descending the funniest thing on the rope
the folding of the blind
'a sense of my vocation that I didn't stop eating.'

Many autobiographers never refer
to their physical appearance at all.
An ardor for everything is reductive

'like a mountain on the mind.'
The parade exacts application. 'Dog' comes
to mean the sound of lapping or padding.

Molten lead dropped into the cool liquid forms
suddenly into shot. The sugar surrenders.
And clouds over crowd a parallel cast.

Many stains on the street
absolved of likeness
always with the same interest because I forget each time.

The horizon is a leading point
an instinct that splits
enthusiasms—Five Weeks in a Balloon—hospitable.

The paragraph is a time unit.
The pint is not a pound
a prone 'world in pictures.'

Published in *Box Car* 1 (1983)
Paul Vangelisti and Leland Hickman, editors

1983

Paradise

Someplace has a history
whose exaggeration is original
... she has an apple
She listens to the music piously

Paradise

Crave adjacency when you spin
Irritation, closely jointed someplace, has a history
Only the sense of motion is enough
Paradise is brown and green and gray
Seclusion is a perfect defeat
Describe pragmatic serpentines
Compare strict shadows, intimate unease
The fear of death is a printed label
A sticky pack of granites, garish with infinity
Rocks in a field form separate scenes
A double life settles over the erotic element
Lighting the way with flaming paper bags
I had the run of a beige couch
Who wouldn't swear to a blank page repeats

Published in *Feminist Studies*, vol. 11, no. 1 (spring 1985)

1983

Magdalena outlines
mathematics amply
Della Della is
garrulous in collaboration
Plenitude is transformed
by long routines

The Proposition

    trace of grapple
    cat trill warbling
    in dark herself
    on lap wobbles echoes
    trinket

1983

taining be tinues
                  move even more I know mostly, mostly so
ball noun music

The Proposition

    per works bird
    the rose gives

1983

hat over ears, therefore muffled and loud, panting
vague crowded—hat!
for your nape
and blue

The Proposition

    the first doodling do
    during grammar
    25 or less
    swords

1983

how patience as soap a tourist heart
of a wedge like a step
from all the people of
the falls bolt guess-works tilted
backward on a defamation, apart
and the night jumps

Critical Essays

The Proposition as Preamble: Lyn Hejinian's Conative Realism
Charles Altieri

> Thinking is about following the dictates of a
> structure calls forth this extension the deep emotions
> of including hope, elation, doubt, despair, and
> uncertain but restless.
>
> . . . Things fall some of the way
> out into the street a new scene. A grid
> worn by water from one place to another. The erosion
> of rocks washed away. The theater of holes dug for trees.[1]

Modernist avant-gardes, even those that seem now arriérre garde, offer their strongest rationales in terms of what they oppose. This is in part because they are still in the process of discovering what this opposition will produce. I want to approach Lyn Hejinian's *The Proposition* under this rubric for two reasons. First her early poetry offers a brilliant defining of what in her mind a new poetry has to reject. And, more important, I think we see in what she builds from these rejections a plausible model for her subsequent work. That work will vary and complicate the model I propose in various interesting ways. But underlying these ways there is a poetics based on what I call a "conative realism." "Conative" stems from Spinoza's idea that every animate being tries to protect and extend a space of intimate engagement where it

The Proposition

can elaborate the powers that have been conferred upon it. Then on the basis of this concern for the conative, Hejinian can elaborate the realism she discusses in her preface. This realism is not based on representations of something external to language but is anchored in qualities of feeling for the deployment of efforts to establish habitation in moments of maximal happening. Consciousness comes to exist in this orienting ourselves toward the real and in caring how those moments can be realized. Such concerns obviously point to the possibility of poetry establishing one important version of such a realism because its basic concerns go beyond accurate naming. Much of our best poetry is concerned primarily with the kinds of activity that can make the real appear in its potential for satisfying the desires that it elicits.

Let me elaborate the passages which serve as my epigraphs in order to illustrate both of my reasons for beginning with Hejinian's understanding of the task of any avant-garde in the arts. For this purpose we have to begin by asking what is rejected because of these attitudes and what is offered in the place of those missing elements. The first feature is the absence of overt subjectivity: no speaker is trying to establish intimate bonds with the audience or expressing how personal feelings pervade the made object. When emotions are present, as in the second epigraph, they are abstract and generic, so that they depend on linguistic effects to take on animation. There is also no fascination with the qualities of discrete objects characteristic of much lyric poetry. There is talk of "things," but it is the abstract terms like "scene," and "Grid," and "erosion," and "theater" that come to the foreground. Things matter, yet resonance resides in what they do in conjunction rather than what they are in themselves. And the reference to theater ultimately affords a startling new context by which to observe holes dug for trees—as if language could transform a discrete set of details into a significant event.

Finally, we have to recognize in these examples how the lack of expressive subjectivity imposes severe demands on the work language has to accomplish. Without a pronounced will controlling the expression, the language in these poems has to rely on foregrounding its own resources. Hejinian's goal seems to be the production of structural relations that enable a dense realization of particular moments in more economical and ideologically less problematic ways than she finds in contemporary poems more bound to traditional expressivist ideals. Notice the density of o sounds that provides the stage for the work "holes" does as the focal point of the poem. Notice too the final adjectival clause that uses a form indistinguishable from a verb in order to establish a complex relationship between absence in the present and potential presence in the future. These bits of language take on intimate energies because of how they build on surprise as their way of gaining access to the evocation of feeling. One good example of this is the list of emotions in the first epigraph concluding with a distortion of syntax that literally manifests what restless uncertainty does to our assumptions about order and grace.

I

I think many of us have learned to appreciate how poets refusing the pleasures of focusing on the expressive subject rely instead on the intricacies of syntactic and aural structures.[2] But Hejinian may be distinctive in how she motivates these movements of language by establishing for them complex emotional and temporal structures. This is why I will spend the rest of this essay trying to define conative realism as a way of demonstrating the intricate senses of intentionality, desire, and projected satisfaction that Hejinian continues to develop throughout her career. Let me concentrate on her briefest poem in order to characterize the core of the conceptual field I want to explore. Then I will develop four basic characteristics distinctive to Hejinian's sense of the kinds of relations in space and in time that make present aspects of emotional and self-reflexive values that are not available in more conventional modes of lyricism.

The example I have chosen haunts me with its emotionally laden abstract suggestiveness:

The Proposition

>   everything'll
>   if everything'ld (p. 101)

This poem depends for its power on locating the dynamic qualities of three absences and filling them in imaginatively in order to provide a present tense for the abstract form that the poem embodies. The invitation to imagining uses and contexts for this language provides something close to a universal model exemplifying how grammatical forms can structure intimate psychological states. In effect each gap solicits readers to explore their own affective investments in possible ways of organizing and completing sentences. And each effort at filling the gaps redirects language toward some segment of what might engage the real if the sentence can be completed.

How can we provide the psychic states that will complete the relationships suggested by putting these lines together? I want to begin with 'If" because there is probably no richer conjunctive force. "If" suggests a structure of intimate interdependency. There is nothing of the loose permissiveness of "and" as conjunction nor the straightforward opposition of "but" and, more complexly, of "yet." And "if" distributes that interdependence both causally and temporally—that is, it implies a "because" and a "when." So the mind must be fully involved. It must establish contextual links that project into a yet unknown but desired future.

"If everything" is a daunting phrase because of its postulated scope. That ambitiousness makes it difficult to fill in the absences. But the difficulty in turn offers the positive possibility of engaging in psychological stakes with a similar scope. In this case it seems wise to begin with the concluding phrase because it indicates that the missing elements have to be verbs. I think of "could" and "would" as obvious candidates. Each leads in a direction at least initially opposed to the other: "could" is a term based on something allowing permission for some action, while "would" invokes a subjective, and subjunctive, state of possible willed complicity.

The union of these two states is possible; indeed that union is the core of conative poetics. Here we can establish an

The Proposition *as Preamble*, by Charles Altieri

evocative relation between the two sentences in three different ways, each implying an entire dispositional state. If a verb is called for in the first line, "will" and "shall" fit the bill nicely, each varying the tone. (But adjectives can also fit. Indeed possibilities proliferate—"still," "full," even "ill." If we focus on "still," we can take advantage of the double meaning of still as temporal adverb and spatial adjective so that the uses match the conjunctive forces of "should" and "could.") And the poem could also present a wary and somewhat uneasy dialogue where people protect themselves from asserting anything definite.

The important principle here is that the poem embodies an abstract yet specific psychological relation between an effort to establish a sense of subjective possibility and the need to correlate this with a recognition of *what can be objectively permitted*. Indeed, we have to take the predicate "everything" very seriously so that we appreciate how grammar extends well beyond human subject-predicate pairings. Hejinian chooses not to render this sense of permissions dramatically as an objective scene because attention would then be placed on specific characters and situations. By abstracting the relationship and inviting readers to produce their own drama, she makes visible how we might choose to define our own versions of recurrent features of experience. We then feel ourselves committed subjects who have to recognize that whatever we choose we are acting within widely shared structures. *We* seem free, but this freedom demonstrates our entanglements in logical necessities.

II

It is not a huge exaggeration to assert that this short poem opens up most of the features of what I want to elaborate as conative realism. Conative realism refers to states in which we feel the presence of a will that orients subjectivity to the world while also recognizing and celebrating how the world defines our "shoulds" and our "woulds." Put more philosophically, Hejinian recognizes from the start of her career that a realism stressing description is terribly limited because it cannot explore the ways psychology and language position what we honor as "real." Conversely, just stressing the subject's linguistic powers submits us to the same limitation at the opposite pole. We are trapped in individual subjectivity, where many of the mysterious workings of language get lost—workings that reveal ideology, introduce opportunities for playfulness or speculation, and invite attention to the formal and structural dependencies accompanying any assertion. Conative realism seeks to abstract from the psychological subject the conditions of desire that make orientations toward the real irreducible features of cognitive experience. And at the same it seeks to open up our senses of the real by correlating observation with all kinds of desires—from playful elaboration to the exploration of how details relate to one another as they are given identities in language.

Now let us test how the concept of conative realism helps us appreciate various features of the writing in *The Proposition*. The first major attribute of conative realism is its distinctive situating of the subject as it orients itself toward the world. That positioning becomes the source of affects both toward the objects of attention and with regard to how the agency imagines possible consequences. In Hejinian's terms, "Experiencing" becomes "an expansive existential commitment: conscious existing as a made and making proposition." (p. xx). "Made" refers to the shape of the proposition as an intervention in the world. And "making" calls our attention to the fact that what is made involves a continuing activity of orientation and then care for what results from the angle of access. The combination of "made" and "making" affords the possibility of "a moment of habitation, created not by a subject (here presumably the poet), but by another, the presence (and hence presentness) of someone or something else" (p. xvi).

In order to appreciate this feeling of habitation in *The Proposition* it is best to look at a poem like "the Integrity." This poem deploys the grammatical resources of "as" in order to articulate the complex states of conative agency involved in two interrelated conditions of experience—recognizing that something is made and appreciating how the sense of presentness involved in tracing the effects of that making allow the moment to project into the future:

> as one goes, along
>
> and given
> a balance that integrates aspects
>
> as — the best one can do —
> all that one knows
>
> in some words
>
> ... got to keep my sense of it, that looking up and lingering over ... the conditional and the whole, careful of expression ... as sound is gathered, with what befalls one, an opening ... in a wind, say, or the ear, as a measure, of style, as of the landscape,
> seen here. (p. 60; the poem "the Points" p. 62 has significant parallels)

The opening "as" sets the stage by activating the adverbial dimensions marking temporal relations with what one might call the modal force that introduces feelings of going along. Then the poem can focus on the kinds of feeling able to frame efforts at keeping the balance for the dimensions, so that the situation allows confidence in a making capable of generating a knowing. Most striking here is the poem's acknowledging the effort involved, especially in the sense of gathering that constitutes habitation. Such gathering offers the reward of producing self-consciousness about what can be involved in its acts of attention. The absorption is so thorough that the final two uses of "as" locate the modal center not in the speaker but in the style making the landscape visible "here." And "here" here is the perfect term of habitation because it refers to the activity of the poem, the self-conscious state of

The Proposition

affirmed authorship, and the qualities of the landscape that tie the states together.

III

Should Hejinian try to establish those qualities more concretely? Or does it suffice just to name the landscape because the work of the poem concerns the state of habitation and not fascination with individual qualities that might be seen? We can better appreciate Hejinian's decision here if we turn to a second feature of conative realism—its ways of staging what language can make available in order to enhance our engagement in conditions defining a world beyond the ego. I speak of conditions because again "here" is the crucial operator. The feeling of orienting to a given situation involves a good deal more than offering accurate descriptions. One might say that it can involve every state of awareness that "habitation" solicits.

Habitation for Hejinian involves a particular understanding of the process of indexing. An index is not a description so much as a way of placing the mind in relation to a "revelatory logic" (p. xii): "It's an account of returns—reiterations as they register differences in the endlessly changing and proliferative contexts in which they recur" (p. xvi). Words discover the world because "the words are the shore between two natures. We make them that they meet" (p. 119).

The poem "For Rae" enacts some of the qualities basic to such indexing:

> is making visible
> this looking out
> the inner is never far away
> who, says which flower is in the field, of whose words
> with one abrupt bud sunbeaming bucket, that quick!
> as make true returns make visible. (p. 110)

Making something visible is not just pointing something out. Pointing indicates an existence but does not usually produce a visibility worth noticing as visibility. Hejinian tries to make visibility visible by having the first line invite a complex state of self-consciousness trying to hold two quite different possibilities in mind. This initial assertion could be read as a question, "is the making visible." Or it could suggest an unnamed (and probably unknown) agency in the subject position of the sentence that works to make visible "this looking out." If we identify with this relation between interrogation and predication, we find ourselves in a good position to appreciate what is involved in conative realism. For it is highly likely that there is no orientation toward the world that is not generated by some kind of uncertainty. Here the uncertainty resides in how looking out can coexist with self-consciousness of playing a role in a making of the scene, and a making of the poem.

Notice how it is the inner that speaks—not a subject but an aspect of subjectivity that invites identification. Yet this identification is not a direct result of empathy. It consists in a simple delight in what the inner gives to the outer, just as the flower that established the sun-bucket is insistently enmeshed in the making power of language. Yet despite this stress on making, there is no idealism nor a solipsism that invites skepticism about idealist stances. Instead there is the strange confident assertion of what is released by the figure of the "sunbeaming bucket." "That quick!" blends a sense of vitality with sudden emergence—thus affirming two basic qualities of what is indexed. And the exclamation point indicates what stakes the spirit might find in such emergence. The "as" in the final line complicates the picture in at least two ways. Its adverbial dimension stresses visibility as an emergent force. And its modal use suggests that feeling need not be focused entirely on the object. Here repetition proposes an intensification of how making visible can work because echoing the first line offers a sense of framed time: attention to the present extends its effects on the spirit and provides a shape for making that extends how visibility can grasp relationships. "Returns" functions as a subject in this sentence.

IV

This intricacy of interwoven elements deserves separate treatment as a third aspect of conative realism because it is so central in Hejinian's poetry from the beginning. One might ask how else her work could so elaborately emphasize the difference between disclosure and description.

This concern for that difference is most sharply realized negatively in her comments on obsolescence, and positively in her working out what "relationality" can become in poetry. For writers identifying with the avant-garde, obsolescence takes many forms. Hejinian finds it most disturbing in our culture's persistent fascination with "received forms" (p. xix) of picturing objects and atmospheres in nature. In her eyes picturing tends to become a process of prettifying what people already know. And when they think they know, they ignore surrounding elements, or the pressure of context, or affective complexities in situations indexed, or all three. In order to break this habit, and its reliance on metaphor, she asserts that "two things added together do not produce a third thing but a relation" (P61).

This seems a simple assertion. But think of Modernist emphases on juxtaposition that try to produce this third independent thing and you will see how radical she is in her efforts to establish a new realism. And it does not hurt that she is so eloquent on the point—both in her preface and in her poetry. Hejinian's original Preface speaks of an intricate relationality reformulating our sense of context in order to provide "a polymorphous relation to the real". Relations herd things not into categories but into structures of "flow and fixity". Such structures highlight various dimensions of scenes not recognized by traditional realism. For example there is the capacity of linguistic syntax to "exhibit constructive, intensifying, and contextualizing powers" as conditioning forces; and subjectivity enters "in its disarray, its ability to play, pretend, or even metamorphose, and in its disappearance from the scene

The Proposition as Preamble, by Charles Altieri

altogether" (p. xviii). Subjectivity need not seek mastery by means of the mind's capacity to produce order. Instead subejctivity can distribute what Malevich called "the additional element" which delights in elaborating relations rather than interpreting them. One mode of such delight consists in stressing how acts of language can complicate context by stressing a forceful "materiality . . . bearing the recombinatory potential of letters, morphemes, and phonemes" (p. xviii). Just recall what the o sounds add the composition of the scene in my second epigraph.

I find the best brief example of extending context by suggestions shaped in large part by linguistic materiality in this short untitled poem:

places
a rain
passes

May's grass
now I guess (p. 84)

Suppose we draw from the dense play of sibilant sounds the possibility that this poem wants to demonstrate and exemplify how we might think about the many ways we can imagine activities involving passage—from intricate spatial linkages, to an ordered temporal flow, to what writing affords as process and as substance. "Places" works as plural noun and present tense verb—again instancing Hejinian's fascination with linking time and space. That dual reference does not establish a third thing but makes present an enduring relation between situations and the activities that bring them to attention. Then we have to ask why this context might call for the verbal formulation "a rain" rather than "the rain." One possible answer is simply that Hejinian has nominalist tendencies that go in fear of universals. But there is here also matter for the ear. "The rain passes" stresses the event of the rain. "A rain passes" is more indefinite about the rain so that the emphasis gets placed on "passes." And "passes" then can do a marvelous job of placing the rain in both spatial and temporal frameworks. This rain has to be seen as fluid and moving from place to place. And this rain does not last very long. All these almost visible aspects of the rain occur because of grammatical density and not because of painterly acumen.

But why the concluding two lines? First, they return us to place, this time in a seasonal framework. "May's grass" can be the object of the verb "passes." And "May's grass" is also not primarily description. The name of the season is established by the first stanza's referring to a rain that passes easily and defines the places that it blesses. "Now I guess" at first seems contradictory: we do not guess about the present tense. But we do guess about what present tense we might be referring to. Here in order to intensify the s sounds "I guess" also produces a different sense of "now" that need not refer to any present but the imagination's desire to occupy this place. In this intellectual context the brevity of the poem also becomes resonant because, in contrast to the often tedious labors of poets and painters, there is so little verbal making needs to produce effects signifying May.

V

My third aspect of conative realism extends the moment into relational space. My fourth aspect extends it into complex elements of temporality created by the structure of conative desire. Hejinian at her best manages to combine the directedness of orientation that shapes expectation with a sense of projection involving a vision of future satisfaction. We can best summarize why this temporality matters for poetry by contrasting it to the kinds of epistemic intentionality elaborated by Edmund Husserl. Husserl needs intentionality in order to treat possibilities of knowing as answers to questions that define needs and perspectives. Conative intentionality, by contrast, projects beyond asking and answering questions by engaging concerns for why these questions originate and how the knowledge gained may issue in various feelings of satisfaction or disappointment. The process of orienting to the world includes senses of "what might be and what might have been" (P122). In both cases what emerges is a "resemblance not coincidence" (P138) that expands in all directions.

"Sending" is a long and difficult poem focused precisely on these issues of extending the space and the time created by efforts to engage the real at any given moment. Here I can only cite the most relevant passages in order to indicate how Hejinian wants continually to open the relational spaces afforded by intense observation. Then I will turn to "It rained all afternoon" in order to trace concrete means by which her poems expand our sense of time as a dynamic concern basic to engaging in the real world.

I begin with a passage from "Sending" on the inadequacies of our commitments to knowing as picturing:

> the restless language
> for knowing, it is
> partial; the extension
> of time is sent history
> and the real present
>
> ... Thinking is about following the dictates of a
> structure calls forth this extension the deep emotions
> of including hope, elation, doubt, despair, and
> uncertain but restless. (p. 116)

Here it is not sufficient to say "what might be, what might have been." There is simply not sufficient satisfaction in our typical ways of knowing. At the least, the poem has to define what is lacking. That definition consists primarily in a contrast between thinking as picturing and thinking as a kind of dwelling focused by emotional forces. It is crucial that we not follow up by trying to attach nouns to these forces. This is why Hejinian ends a list of names for emotions by shifting to adjectives at the end. And these adjectives combine domains, shifting from the epistemic term uncertain to the behavioral term "restless."

This shifting gets more concrete, and more complex, as the poem turns toward the end to stress how the ocean might sponsor kinds of thinking.

The Proposition

> . . . A full ocean and the seven thoughts suddenly respond
> yet always extend through the years
>   The possible thoughts or the full years always extend
> but legibly return in an ocean . . .
>   The words are the shore between two natures. We
> make them that they meet. The share we have not
> even begun to examine is the ransom and damnation. . . .
>   The sun is not kept out but shines on the
> extension of a, library, year set in motion,
> went constantly between what's known and what's
> to know. (pp. 117–18)

Hejinian repeats "extend" for good reason. Reference to the ocean cannot quite be localized: it is always more than we can actually see, and it breeds analogies and reflections that extend from memory into projections about future possibilities. Words become the shore that enables focus on parts of the ocean, but we always know that this state of observation is a part of a more expansive process. One of these expansions is to shift to the sun that is often in the background when we think ocean. In fact we do not just make propositions about the sun. The object of the proposition becomes the subject eliciting further propositions by means of its shining. Given this relation, we have to recognize that because words are "a shore between two natures" we are constantly torn between the sense of redemption when the shore gets populated with what we desire and the sense of damnation when the shore has to let its barrenness become visible and perhaps inevitable.

   Such passages effectively make Hejinian's general case about the place of emotions in cognitive activity. But we need to understand how the differences are spreading within processes where specific concerns fold into one another and shape possible satisfactions. "It rained all afternoon," for example, traces the emergence of a future built on careful attention to how we can see the present in its full particularity:

> It rained all afternoon. Plots abut
>   the milk of glass leveled along an oblong

The Proposition as Preamble, by Charles Altieri

    green. The glare throws shadows in odd directions.
        shakes the distinctive shimmer. The sky removes
  absolutism with changing moods, of wool and gold.

  A dirty secondary heap has for its object
     mutual assistance. A link with the staggering store
       is forged. The minimally knotted walls prop
  the description. Specifically the general type
    is pierced by its phenomena. . . .

                . . . One sees
    how they come out.

  The dogged sunniness shines. The light scatters
    shadows it could cloud over the corner.
  A mall, slim, abuts the public sidewalks.
  Vacant lots, money aprons, prostrate trunks portion
    off the shore. (p. 152)

It is stunning to me how deftly Hejinian surprises with her choices in sound play and diction so that poetry can have a distinctive form of internal richness despite its refusal of metaphor or clear story line. I lack a language by which to generalize about her alternative. But I can point out some stunning effects. Consider the use of "abut" to place plots within the activity of attending to the scene without displacing it into an expressive structure foregrounding the author's sensibility. Instead "abut" seems a striking term for giving plots a power to occupy space. Then the concluding sentence of the first stanza insists that the sky, as we have just seen with the sun, can play the role of subject breaking up any absolutism that would fix a scene as exemplary. The sky possesses a density of color that has to be aligned with the psyche's various moods: exchange runs rampant and produces a sense of time aligned with vision and with touch. And then there is the sound play deepening the poem's sense of fusion between the work of mind and the satisfactions of the eye. Changing moods as contexts for viewing the sky are literally grounded in the opening play on o sounds and the rich monosyllabic assonance that concludes the stanza.

The second stanza turns from the sky to a "dirty secondary heap." We need not have a description of that heap. What matters is its effect on sensibility while relying on evocation without traditional metaphor. "Mutual assistance" here consists largely in how the details play on a relation between actual phenomena like the knotted walls in what seem to be intricate patterns and the general type evoked in what is elicited by the heap. Changing moods in, or of, the sky frame a particular object whose resistance to expectations of pleasure evokes an abstract sense of need for mutual assistance. Then Hejinian turns to a final play between the categorical and the particular. The sun returns, insisting on a "dogged" presence, with "dogged" playing the anti-metaphoric role of specifying the concrete effects of what mood can do. And sunshine per se becomes far less important than tracing how the light illuminates the shadows. This allows an expansion of the scene—both physically and visually as the shore comes to seem intimately a part of the town. And this portioned off shore ultimately marks a boundary that projects into possible futures. Light and shadow cannot be reduced to the single scene in which they work in the present.

VI

Hejinian is rarely explicit in these poems about how the work they do correlates with the intense rendering of claims for poetry's powers to produce senses of sociality offered in her preface. But if we concentrate on how these poems dramatize the powers of conative thinking, we can see them seeking to provide alternatives to a world of raging ideological conflict. Think of how they stress versions of subjective agency carried by language not individual genius, of how this benign impersonality extends access to a world framed by all sorts of relations beyond those that establish belief in facts, of how making these relations visible is much less a matter of the poet's will than of the poet's feel for what making can do to share what sensibility discloses, and of how that making can come to align with social spaces that are simply there—like our lives—without any signs of self-congratulation or self-delusion. This book presents a set of beginnings that have proven capable of sustaining a lifelong project of showing to ourselves who we can be when we embed ourselves in what dailiness affords.

Notes

1. Lyn Hejinian, *The Proposition*, pp. 116, 145. Subsequent references to this work will be in the main text prefaced by P throughout the essays.
2. For superb poetry criticism in this vein see Craig Dworkin, *Radium of the Word: A Poetics of Materiality* (Chicago: University of Chicago Press, 2020) and Marjorie Perloff, *Infrathin: An Experiment in Micropoetics* (Chicago: University of Chicago Press, 2021).

Early Hejinian
Lytle Shaw

One of the opportunities offered by the publication of Lyn Hejinian's *The Proposition* is to trace in it, in nascent form, many of the key concerns of the poet's later, better-known work. As we read the longer poems, for instance, we notice the sudden shifts from playful quotidian, often meta-linguistic observations, to more direct philosophical claims—claims about how poetry takes on meaning, and also about how statements and thinking more generally do so. What emerges here is not only the project of doing rigorous poetics, but also the characteristic interweaving of that poetics within what we might think of as poetry proper. Or rather, not quite proper, because if theory bubbling up inside poetry was an affront to many conceptions of the field in the 1960s and 1970s (as it still is), so, in a different way, was the range of writing modes that might count as the baseline of experimental poetry for Hejinian at the time: punning neologisms ("hushabye," "dawnple," "altared") that subtend an exploration, in the "Adam of the Animals," of the "spell" (in the dual sense of casting a spell and constructing a word, letter by letter); reflexive attention to the threshold between poetry and everyday language "not yet separated from the world // 'to fill pages'"; and wildly fragmentary short poems, like this one, comprised only of two lines: "everything'll / if everything'ld"

In this last, poetry's confident Adam of spells seems to have fallen prey to one. Here Hejinian's frequent evocation of the West and even the western takes on something of the mood of Robert Altman's *McCabe and Mrs. Miller*, where the tough cowboys of yore who barked unambiguous commands above the tumbleweeds have, in the psychedelic late-1960s, grown self-conscious and now test comments subvocally in the corners of darkened barrooms. We get another variant on this psychotropic landscape in the *Grreat Adventure*, which begins: "there is this love I want to lay on you / ace man in green jeans / from a skinface mama." I do not believe any subsequent Hejinian poems involve the phrase "lay on you," especially about love offered by a "mama" to an "ace man" whose jeans color the picture, which is then illuminated by the word "electric," and subject to sudden jolts (à la comic book interventions) by the all-caps "BLAM." The adventure offered in this poem (so great that it requires an extra r) seems to oscillate between the outer-space of contemporary moon landings, with the astronaut in his floating module subject to the whims of his inadequate computer infrastructure ("I'm inburning / NOTHING LIKE IT IN THE SIMULATOR / I'm inburning") and the (perhaps surprisingly paired) inner space of high Modernist painterly simulation, in the domestic worlds of Vuillard and Bonnard.

As in Hejinian's later work, there is throughout *The Proposition* a consistent attention to the relation between sense perception and its raw materials: "this letter / is tending (also tender[.]". We begin perhaps by noticing the curve or acute angle of a written character (the direction it points, or tends), and from there project affective associations onto it above and beyond those of literal meaning or practical communication. If words are tenders in the legal sense (abstract offerings that stand in for things, like counters or chips or dollars), their visual and sonic tendencies, the way they lean graphically or sound gradually through repetition, can always also make them tender (or tense) tenders, depending. However much a deeper plunge into "experience" may be a crucial horizon in Hejinian's work, poetry is never less real than life:

The Proposition

"Is anything more 'real' than a poem?" And we get at poetry's reality in part by attention to those aspects of language that exceed or complicate mimesis or functional communication: "Wet tin green-red rings." Hejinian here marshals a set of short (three to five letter) words whose sounds begin to collapse into one another. The vivid visual picture is strangely extended by the line's sonic effects, as if the words too were staining each other with their correlated and overlapping sounds. Elsewhere in the book memorability and vividness emerge through a more conceptual orientation: "One more day less." The oxymoronic makes space for the plausible as the positive and negative valences of time counting first cancel and then make room for each other. Something similar emerges with "I grin out as shoppers pass from nothing to nothing more." Accounting for this situated viewpoint from which shoppers appear and then disappear, Hejinian plays both on their sudden emergence "from nothing" and on their not quite parallel passage into history or memory—"nothing more." Once gone, they are nothing any more. But this second nothing is not quite parallel, since it carries with it the trace of a vanished experience, the "more" that is not exactly a more of nothing, even though it is a nothing more.

At times, the pursuit of vivid sense perception takes on a different kind of self-reflexivity: "These pages flame with amorous adventures, flanked by blanks moved back." Though these flaming pages might be taken to evoke literal intercourse, strangely the more immediate—more vivid—sense of this adventure is our experience of these very words, as they flame out onto the page and move back the blanks (the white space of unprinted potentiality) that flank them. This line perhaps becomes a theme song or microcosm for *The Proposition*—a cue to pay close attention to the drama of these printed letters rushing onto the page, a troupe of character actors coalescing briefly into and dissipating after a sequence of short, abstract poems.

And yet, anyone attentive to Hejinian's reception will note the strangeness of an account of her work (like mine so far) focusing entirely at the scale of the individual line—that is, independent of the architecture of the project: the serial poem whose organizational structure guides us so that, however disjunctive or multivalent the individual lines, still we feel we have some footing within the larger structure of the book. Despite the fact that *The Proposition* does include a number of longer poems (among them, "The River Nets the Peninsula," "*The Grreat Adventure*," "A Month Without Days," "Chronic Texts," and "Sending"), these poems are neither modular components within a single unified book-project, nor the dominant mode of writing in the collection.[1] So there is something refreshingly strange in encountering a group of short Lyn Hejinian poems that do not arrive within larger conceptual architectures; they are not part of a serial poem whose divisions give it pacing, structure, analogical links to time. In some sense, Hejinian has not arrived at what will become her dominant mode—if, that is, we think of her work in relation to the larger conceptual architecture by which she will structure longer works like *My Life* (1980), *A Border Comedy* (2001), or *Slowly* (2002)—to choose but three of Hejinian's many longer serial works. There is not, of course, one Hejinian "project." But there is in her work from the mid-1970s on the sense that each book gathers part of its meaning from its larger structure of organization: most famously, *My Life* (1980, with its first edition comprised of thirty-seven sections, one per year of her life at that point, each section built out of thirty-seven sentences). This is certainly also the case with books such as *Writing is an Aid to Memory* (1978, with its arrangement of lines across the page—ones beginning with A words at far left, Z at far right) where the page becomes a kind of mnemonic landscape, patterned alphabetically; *Oxota* (1991, with its 270 sonnets in dialog with Pushkin's *Eugene Onegin*); and *A Border Comedy* (2001, with its fifteen books organized around the border between timeless concepts and contingent examples). Similar conceptual and organizational frames could be cited for almost all of her books. One of their central effects, again, is the perhaps illusory sense that we can plug otherwise wayward or recalcitrant observations into these structures, that such larger frames make us feel a bit

The Proposition

more comfortable about the often wildly anarchic particulars of Hejinian's ongoing writing. This framing effect, however, is not only a product of her books' conceptual structures; it's also a result of Hejinian's powerful writing in poetics, by which I mean that component of her work that announces itself as criticism. Hejinian's influential essay "The Rejection of Closure" was first published in 1983; *The Language of Inquiry* came out in 2000 and will soon be supplemented by *Allegorical Moments*. These essays are of course also in dialog with works of poetics associated with Language writing. In these contexts, a book of Hejinian's poetry could almost always be discussed in relation to a series of powerful frames: it was a book-length, serial poem, involved with, or structured around, an explicitly announced way of organizing its lines or parts. Further, it was "Language writing." And we know what this is, right? One perhaps questionable way critics have demonstrated this knowledge is by turning her works into quarries for illustrating her propositions—reading, that is, top-down, from the propositions and organizational mechanisms to the details, so that the lines exemplify the larger "ideas." Given the complexity of Hejinian's proposals about poetics, the extreme variety and density of her writing, and perhaps even the concern that certain lines of thinking inside a single work may not always reconcile themselves easily with others, it is understandable that critics have often turned to her claims in poetics. The question (posed freshly by this new publication) becomes how one takes her poetic writings seriously without using them to contain her works' generative strangeness. Part of what's fascinating about these newly published poems is to imagine trying to make sense of them at the moment of their composition—that is, before the larger infrastructure of Language writing was entirely built.

One might plausibly imagine that Hejinian herself saw the larger framing structures as useful counterweights to the contingency of many individual lines, that employing them allowed her to describe the books in clearer ways, and that in both of these senses the move to this scale tightened the work conceptually and made it feel more rigorous. All of this seems reasonable in a way. As she puts it at one point in this book: "I want harder reasons." And yet, there may be a real advantage in at least temporarily suspending what we think we know about Hejinian's poetics, and about Language writing. *The Proposition*, as a work without much of this larger organizational architecture, might help us do so, as we dive into the anarchic texture of its micro-events. The point would not be simply to forget Hejinian's rich terms and organizational structures and celebrate a series of microlinguistic occurrences ostensibly on their own, independent of larger contexts. The specific, small language event is not more authentic than the larger frame in poetics, and anyway can't exist on its own indefinitely. If it is going to be of use, the instance must ultimately give rise to other characterizations of the project. Thus, the opportunity offered by *The Proposition* might better be understood in relation to something like the methods of microhistory, where case studies that develop exceptions to dominant historiographic arguments ultimately give rise to more interesting arguments. Why *The Proposition* provides this opportunity, then, is both that it was composed (for the most part) prior to the development of a dominant Language writing poetics, and it is comprised (also for the most part) of small units without what I've described as conspicuous organizational architecture.

Let us return to the singular drama of written characters rushing onto the white sheets of paper.[2] Consider how the following nine-word poem flames into view, as the surrounding blanks move back:

places
a rain
passes

May's grass
now I guess

In a sense this poem takes place in the space between two sets of similar words: places and passes; grass and guess. The first pair seems primarily to operate by contrast, as the rain might pass the places that stay still. We can imagine a fixed view of a few of these places that then begins to move, and follow the rain, as it passes. Or we can just imagine the rain moving out of view. In the second stanza, the silent suggestion of the April shower now underlies the rhyming May's grasses, which spins on May flowers. As we move from grasses to guesses, the poem's "I" now perhaps imagines a causality for the emergence of these grasses, which links the two stanzas, and also positions the guessing as a form of mental irrigation that now has a strange parallel to the rain. Though I've just composed a paragraph about these nine words, what really fascinates me about them is not so much the images suggested or the structures of distorted parallelism that seem to emerge from related but slightly different words. No, what most fascinates me about a piece of writing like this is how it seems to sit *just barely* over the threshold that might separate poetry from everyday language. We still have a sense of these words operating as they were before, a sense that poetry's organization of them is only tentative and temporary, provisional.[3]

Though they are now on the page, these nine words have not been moved too far from what they were doing before Hejinian noticed them, noticed certain possibilities for connecting them. Many of the words in *The Propositions* are like this, leading their quiet lives close by, minding their own business, until they are nominated to become poetry. They were words that were nominally functional, but also words (as all are) with sonic or graphic tendencies and residues that might begin to function in totally non-functional ways, newly flaming across pages, pushing back blanks. In one sense, *The Proposition* is about this shift in context, from use to reflexive contemplation. But there is also an exemplary dimension to the project that exceeds the examples presented here and invites us to think more broadly, on our own terms, about the threshold between everyday words and the forms of arrangement that might conscript them to function as poetry.[4]

If Hejinian can be considered a quotidian poet—and I think she can—still she introduces already in this early book basic complications to such poetry's frequently more confident moods about presence and immediacy: "I see that I live instantly but in retrospect". Rather than simply understand temporality as undermining instantaneity, she proposes it here as the content of the always vanishing present. Words are subject to similar destabilizations. The poems offer patient and playful attention to how words focalize and mediate experience; but they also pause, at times, to note alien vortices that open up inside the seemingly simplest ones. "*Hug* and *lunch*: both are words which become strange when repeated." Repetition casts a spell that gradually obliterates "what they signify" and amplifies instead their "look and sound," which in turn signify in unpredictable and uncontrollable ways. Experimentation with the terms and effects of the spell of repetition will, of course, structure considerable parts of Hejinian's subsequent work.

Ditto gaps. The book focuses attention on the often-missing connections between Hejinian's sentences or lines, the logical and referential leaps necessary to connect details or propositions in her poems, which have of course been a central concern for Hejinian's later critics. Gaps are often physicalized in *The Proposition*: people fall into the empty spaces between ships and shores, horses and fields, farms and buried cities. They fall out of moving vehicles and through doors. Sometimes these unwitting micro-characters are then dragged or hurt themselves in other ways as they're pulled through meta-narrative anecdotes that evoke what Barthes calls the novelesque without the novel. "For Rodney had suffered a head wound while discovering an immense metal city buried under his farm." But gaps, and the surprises buried in them, are also the occasion for philosophical thinking: "Between one and another what is relation is translation". The problem lurking inside the term "relation," in other words, is that it requires the articulation of common denominators, which in turn necessitates a description of features, and an elevation of some of those features to the point of representativity. To say A is in some way like B is to perform this whole "translation" process—often more or less unconsciously.

The Proposition

Most commonly, this project of calling attention both to the normative conventions and the abyssal problems underlying everyday interpretive acts has been claimed by "theory." It still makes many readers uncomfortable when poetry does it. And yet, if Hejinian is beginning to articulate a poetics in *The Proposition*, if she is testing out a series of concerns that will be developed in works that will soon follow, then these concerns are not just personal themes or leitmotivs that can be used to read her work. They are, I think, better characterized as part of what will be developed both in her work, and in the work of her peers within Language writing, as a theoretical project, one that might be specified further as a widespread analysis of poetry's internal conventions and external contexts, its meaning making mechanisms and its institutional circuits, including criticism and pedagogy. The term "institution" here perhaps evokes the practice of institution critique in art. But while Language writing is explicitly concerned with the social implications of poetry's institutions, it is perhaps less inclined to use the sociological methods often employed in art practice. Language writing's "institution critique" is more concerned with the social implications of formal structures. And forms tend to be understood as potentially various in their effects, rather than uniform and symptomatic. Which makes for a still largely unresolved tension in the understanding even of the group's name: the movement is often associated (rightly) with the post-structural proposition that subjectivities are made out of (rather than simply expressed through) language. The complication comes when critics then too quickly plug in understandings of such making that come out of versions of theory (I'm think of some modes of cultural studies and some components of the Frankfurt School) that see this making in the most instrumental political terms: a one-way pressure that symptomatically imprints. Though we can certainly locate instances of such symptomatic imprinting within Hejinian's work, ultimately she is interested in a far wider array of relations between models of subjectivity and language. And these cannot simply be summarized as a bleak, one-way process of fashioning docile subjects

There are, in *The Proposition* for instance, other possibilities: "everything'll / if everything'ld." What's uncharacteristic and funny about a poem like this (to approach it from a slightly different angle) is the vast amount of space Hejinian allows this ambiguous double conditional statement. We must allow ourselves to be comfortable with its drifting off, without any clear relationship to a larger organizational structure. That is, while Hejinian's later work, too, will play with the threshold between unremarkable quotidian language and poetry, the very fact that such instances are arranged into numerically consistent blocks and patterns in the later work fundamentally changes our relationship to them. This, perhaps, is one component of what's "experimental" about the poems in this book. Though there is some disjunction and semantic overdetermination, the more fundamental concern in *The Proposition* seems to be testing the threshold between everyday language and poetry in short poems that arrive without the frames through which later readers of Hejinian will be taught how to read. Instead, we follow these micro-events of words coming into consciousness as they move along the spectrum from use to mention, from general mention to mention *in* poetry, and from mention *in* poetry to mention *as* poetry. In this sense the title of the book is not only the forward-looking launch of a mode of poetics, but also the very present tense performative act of fastening on words nearby and tracking them across these thresholds. The poems *propose* everyday word clusters as poems, casting our attention on the strangeness and surplus tending of the most ordinary components of our language. I wish there were more poetry books about what words were doing before they became poetry—"not yet separated from the world // 'to fill pages.'"

Notes

1. In this sense the collection is perhaps comparable to *The Cold of Poetry* (Los Angeles: Sun and Moon, 1994), which brought

together ten earlier poems. But even this collection includes entirely serial work, and mostly work from after 1980.
2. Such a characterization will likely call to mind Jerome McGann's later and wonderful argument about the active role of the printed character in Modernist typography in *Black Riders: The Visible Language of Modernism* (1993). Though Hejinian was certainly in dialog with McGann, he almost certainly did not see the unpublished poem, "Short Arbiter," where Hejinian develops this concept.
3. This is perhaps as close as Hejinian gets to Larry Eigner, with whom she was in dialog, and whose book *Flat and Round* she published (through Tuumba) in 1980.
4. We may be jaded, perhaps, by the familiar model of readerly co-production of meaning and its corollary of interpretive play that emerges in part from Roland Barthes and has been frequently cited in accounts of Language writing and the avant-garde more broadly. Fredric Jameson's critique of play in *Postmodernism* suggested that the would-be innocent activity celebrated since German Romanticism was better understood as an early phase in acculturation or training. Among the most fascinating and surprising critiques of the co-production of meaning is one offered by Vito Acconci in his poems of the late 1960s, which invited reader participation only to bureaucratize it into a level of tedium that couldn't *possibly* be mistaken as liberatory. Such critiques to my mind suggest not the inherent poverty of these concepts so much as the need to consider their histories, specify their senses, and not simply value them a priori. Used in such a way, co-production at least has the advantage of suggesting that meaning is not an object to be handed out, a "content," so much as the result of a process whose elements of contingency a reader can acknowledge, or not. If this is a cultic belief of the avant-garde, it is nonetheless one with some functional utility.

Lyn Hejinian's Faustienne Beings-With
Emily Critchley

> Along comes something – launched in context
> In context to pass it the flow of humanity divides and on the
>   other side
>   unites
> All gazing at the stars bound in a black bow
> I am among them thinking thought through the thinking
>   thought to no
>   conclusion'[1]

Since the 1970s Lyn Hejinian has produced a prolific array of cross-genre poetry, poetic prose and poetics that investigate mutually constitutive relationships, including: interplays between poetic, critical and philosophical languages; the nature of perceptual encounters between subject and object; and interrelations between the writer and her context, including her own intellectual background. She has always been concerned with both the 'motivated coincidence[s]'[2] as well as differences within the various literary communities she has inhabited, especially those of Language poetry and the Russian avant-garde.[3] In Hejinian's words: 'To trace the lines of reciprocity through which [meaningfulness and meaning . . .] are established is to map a social space, a community.'[4] Her writing often bears witness to specific occasions that prompted literary activity within these communities, such as readings, talks, calls for papers, translations, and so on, as well as the people with whom she has collaborated or for whom she has written.

Her book of poetics, *The Language of Inquiry*, is a compilation of such papers, talks, correspondences and poems. In its introduction she writes:

> Like George Oppen, I am aware that poets work in the context of 'being numerous.' These essays were prompted by invitations and called into existence by occasions, but their true context is a community – literary and pedagogical – in which challenges and encouragement, provocations and excitement, contention and insights have been generated over the years in a mode which I would define as friendship of the most supreme kind.[5]

Hejinian has long been recognized for her active support of other poets within the experimental community or, better, communities – many of whom she published through her own press, Tuumba, which she ran for eight years (1976–84). She was also joint editor, alongside Barrett Watten, of *Poetics Journal* from 1981 to 1999. She then became co-director of Atelos, a literary project commissioning and publishing a wide variety of cross-genre work. Her encouragement of other female poets in particular, in the form of publications, but also through private letters and emails, is discussed in detail, for instance, by Ann Vickery in *Leaving Lines of Gender*,[6] and by Nicky Marsh who writes of the 'lengthy but largely private' 'battle' that was Hejinian's 'vigorous' attempt 'to make Language writing's literal poetic community aware of the gendering of its own practices'.[7]

Her central place within the Language grouping, arguably unparallelled amongst the female Language writers, was achieved early on in the group's formation due to her active self-identification with and promotion of the practices of that community. For instance, her work shows a major investment in many of the formal, political and philosophical concerns of other Language writers, such as a focus on leftist politics, philosophy and the defamiliarizing literary strategies of poetic predecessors – the Objectivist poets and Gertrude Stein to name two of the most important. Yet, as much as she has always been identified with the Language group, Hejinian's writing resists some of the more extreme or abstract theories of her male Language peers. Instead of denying representation or authorial subjectivity,[8] for example, (as if that were possible) her poetic explorations of notions of the writer's self and the 'lived experience', in phenomenological terms, has given her work a subjective element denounced by some of the other Language writers.[9] Her investigations into subjectivity and, in particular, an 'embedded', female subjectivity – personal and political, actively engaged and intellectual – are especially encouraging to the feminist reader of Language poetry. Her multiple and sometimes conflicting positions as a Language writer, a feminist, an academic, a wife and a mother simultaneously, have meant that Hejinian has lived out, quite literally, most of the different possibilities of ontologically 'being-with'[10] under discussion here. As she explains in her paper 'Language and "Paradise"': 'The parenthetical plural is always part of her condition. And her subject-object, I-we, public-private status becomes ever more pronounced in the "unconventional position" which constitutes the writing posture.'[11]

Much of Hejinian's thinking and writing has focused on dialectical overlaps between the political and personal, or the literary and the lived, both sides of which can be realms of intellectual concern if approached with thorough-going self-awareness. Due perhaps to the need for complex negotiations between different subject positions, her writing has remained resistant to the kind of authoritarian, single-minded or abstract tendencies which Language poetics ostensibly eschewed, but which, as I have explored elsewhere, much of it ended up reproducing.[12] As Hejinian puts it in *My Life in the Nineties*: 'One wants one's work to be shareable – one seeks the shareable (*not* universal).'[13] Instead, she has argued for a poetry of careful epistemology,[14] but one which is radically 'contextual and always shifting'[15] – one that constitutes a specifically *female* mode of thinking, according to Hejinian, which she termed 'La Faustienne'.[16]

Though Hejinian invokes thinking from a wide variety of intellectual movements – especially Language writing and a range of phenomenologies, but also Russian formalism, Objectivism, the Frankfurt School, various feminisms, and so on – she deliberately writes away from any single perspective or totalizing intellectual system, always attempting, instead, to question and transgress the boundaries with which any political or philosophical stance cordons itself off. Consequently, her work is hard to 'fix' critically. Instead, it requires wilful immersion in its suspension of many of the markers of causality, 'aboutness' and value. For Hejinian constantly shifts the boundaries of both content and intent, of inside and outside, in her writing; as she puts it: '"aboutness" (in poetry, but [. . .] also in life) is transitional, transitory'.[17] She has written repeatedly of an ambivalence of intention in both her poetry and her poetics: these being the important spaces, for her, in which encounters with the world, with variant and unforeseen events, including meaning, especially the meaning and meaningfulness of others, can take place. For instance, she writes about how 'the swirl of meaningfulness' which is 'part of the ongoing course of one's daily living among others' only becomes visible within a mode of reduced intentionality, which lets otherness appear.[18]

Writing on Stein's *Stanzas in Meditation* in 'A Common Sense' Hejinian notes that 'there is a difference between thinking *about* and thinking, and thinking itself is meaningful too' (italics mine).[19] Later in the same essay she articulates the specifically phenomenological thrust of this understanding:

> the substance of the [*Stanzas in Meditation* . . .] is the recurrent coming into appearance, the phenomenology, of meanings, the varieties of meanings, the demands of meanings, the endless and difficult meaningfulness that faces one everyday. The meditation is not simply a response to meaning; rather, it is the articulation of being in meaning – in the stream of meaning.[20]

The liquid imagery employed in this essay: 'stream', 'swirl', 'ongoing course', 'rippling effects', may have its roots in what William James repeatedly referred to as 'the stream of consciousness' in his writings – itself an influence on Stein's studies in psychology under James. Elsewhere in 'Two Stein Talks' Hejinian muses on James' analyses of consciousness, though she records her own experience of consciousness as, conversely, 'broken up, discontinuous – sometimes radically, abruptly, and disconcertingly so'.[21] On the other hand, this disjunction between the self and the self experiencing consciousness of the self exists, for Hejinian, within a larger continuum, that of community.

Hejinian's work embraces a Steinian brand of realism, one that is inclusive, not conclusive, as well as vulnerable, shifting and uncertain – based on the ever-changing dynamics of perception itself. Yet such uncertainty, rather than precluding a sense of hope or affirmation is, on the contrary, the very sign of full living for the writer. As she explains in 'Reason', to be lodged in 'doubt', 'dilemma' and self-questioning, is to be on the way to 'affirmation of our deepest reason, the one that tells us that things and our experiences of them count'.[22] Moreover, Hejinian frequently rescues the positive connotations of the word 'ambivalence', denoting not an either/or, but a condition of both, simultaneously. As in the following, from her poem *Slowly*:

> I can't help but yield philosophically to the proliferation of
>   detail, the endless
> distinctions, large and small, deliberately producing
>   contradictions,
> irreconcilability, and, in me, irresolution, so that I can
>   only offer ambivalence happily in place of conviction –
>   evasiveness, prevarication, the presentation of things that are
>   abruptly otherwise . . .[23]

Thus is it necessary for Hejinian to maintain a 'healthy dialectic between poetry and poetics', as she writes in *My Life*,[24] a phenomenological approach that crucially upsets the object relations of traditional, academic analysis, from the perspective of which 'poetry stands at a distance, objectified and under scrutiny'.[25] However, against, in Hejinian's terms,

The Proposition

'the famous (or notorious) postmodern (or postpostmodern) negativity [...] a gap of meaning',[26] her emphasis on perceiving relations *between* and *with* phenomena is always as an activity through which humans can better come to know one another and themselves – a concept she inherited from phenomenologists James, Heidegger, Arendt and Merleau-Ponty, as well as from Stein and Oppen. As the latter wrote:

> There are things
> We live among 'and to see them
> Is to know ourselves' ...[27]

Or as Hejinian puts it in her introduction to *Inquiry*: 'It is at points of linkage – in contexts of encounter [...] that one discovers the reality of *being in time*, of *taking one's chance*, of *becoming another*, all with the implicit understanding that *this is happening*.'[28] Via this intellectual context, as well as Stein's explorations of subjectivity and gender, Hejinian developed a contemporary, feminist poetics of the 'third-wave', i.e., active, political and self-aware, whilst being always contingent, at times contradictory and non-definitive.

In place of rationalistic principles of objectivity and generalizability, Hejinian's writing discovers knowing to be an ongoing activity, a perpetual coming-to-know, or 'not-yet-knowing',[29] characterized by self-questioning, doubt and strangeness, during which the perceiver comes to recognize both the object under perception and herself as 'other'. With reference to what Oppen described as 'O's affirmation': the 'curiosity – "care, concern" – which makes [...] things count', Hejinian describes the activity of mind she calls 'doubt' as 'not entirely unlike what Keats called negative capability';[30] in other words, an intentional open-mindedness that puts us in coexistence with uncertainties and that which cannot be resolved or understood through reason.[31] This sense of being-with or, as Hejinian puts it, 'coinciding' with things, forms the basis of her writing, i.e., the dynamic of our happening to notice things, our coming into coexistence momentarily with them, but stopping short of the need to possess, categorize or contain them.

Such a process of acknowledgement has important ethical connotations because it allows for the affirmation and value of things and persons, such as 'women and other "others"',[32] without submitting them to conceptual objectification (the first stage in hierarchization?). In 'Barbarism', for instance, Hejinian cites an essay by Peter Nicholls on Oppen, entitled 'Of Being Ethical', noting its influence on her own poetics.[33] 'Such a "poetics of encounter"', Hejinian writes, employing Nicholls' phrase, 'has an ethical dimension, since it is established within relationships expressing proximity rather than contemplative or legislative distance'.[34] Modern feminist philosophers such as Carol Gilligan and Martha Nussbaum have understood that the subsection of philosophy entitled ethics has long been grounded in a patriarchal, masculinist definition of 'reason', of the type that Hejinian continually challenges – such as in her essay of the same name.[35] Hejinian's poetics, conversely, tends toward something more like virtue theory,[36] which insists that morality is not about conforming to a set of infallible, objective rules, but about being trained to see problematic situations in a moral way.

The poet's creative explorations along a border of ethics and aesthetics in part accounts for the emphasis on haecceity or 'thisness' throughout her oeuvre (which she shares with Oppen and Stein) in place of symbolic categorizations, because, as she puts it: 'To know *that* things are is not to know *what* they are, and to know *that* without *what* is to know otherness (i.e., the unknown and perhaps unknowable).'[37] To state that 'a rose is a rose is a rose' tells us nothing particularly useful or generalizable about that flower (and yet how much it says about the immediacy of encounter!). It also accounts for the 'spirit of provisionality'[38] in which Hejinian has always written, and the importance to her work of contradiction and paradox. Such a stake in dynamic and contradictory opposites shows the poet's commitment to an alternative dialectics, or processes of 'assimilation', in Hejinian's words, 'where opposites as such can't exist because they always coexist'.[39]

In her essays 'The Quest for Knowledge in the Western poem'[40] and 'La Faustienne' Hejinian explicates a familiar feminist argument that the need to know is, historically, on some level, often a need to contain or possess, and identifies the trail of destruction this dynamic has left in its wake. Both of these essays differently ask the question 'What does a poem know?' and, in the process, identify the search for a 'body of knowledge' as being 'a peculiarly Western construct'.[41] Hejinian offers this body in terms of the conquest of a geographical landmass, specifically Columbus' fabled 'discovery' of America (though he never set foot on American soil), the mythologized Faust's desire to know everything, and the gendered dominance that men have historically sought over women. In so doing, she identifies the quest for 'obtaining and securing' knowledge as the driving force of occidental study for the last thousand or so years.[42]

Her response to such a 'force' in 'The Quest for Knowledge' is to uncover and explore areas of 'unsettlement and disorientation'.[43] Formally, the essay is comprised of poetry intermixed with sections of expository prose based on notes written to parallel the poetry. Such a form is disorienting in itself and in some ways affirms and enacts Hejinian's subject of estrangement from certainty. The focus is on the contingent, culturally constructed nature of knowledge: 'Western knowledge itself has been a set of inventions, framed by perception but linked to anticipation' Hejinian writes.[44] Hence her passion for alternative, non-Western viewpoints. In Hejinian's case, this has been most explicit in her multiple voyées into Russian thinking, writing and translating, which resulted in, amongst other works, *Oxota: A Short Russian Novel*.[45] *Oxota*'s narrator is marked by a sense of dislocation and disorientation, which Hejinian describes in 'The Quest for Knowledge' as 'very much a Russian theme'.[46] Hence too her desire to undercut the 'simulacrum of stability of both locale and self' that, in her view, has reached a damaging peak in the ideational construct of the Western world. As she writes in 'The Person and Description':

The individual is a figure that steadfastly, in Western culture, appears at the apex of hierarchical structures; it stakes its claims on them and establishes itself as their dominating figure [... T]he notion of 'identity' – the identity of the individual – is itself party to a hierarchical structure, one in which 'identity' governs the question of who an individual might be. And yet, even as identity is a governing factor, it is a limiting factor too.[47]

Throughout her work, especially in *A Border Comedy*,[48] *The Cold of Poetry*[49] and *The Cell*,[50] Hejinian reconfigures concepts of person and place, such as the 'I' and 'the West' (referring to the Western world), regularly assumed to be dominant, self-contained entities, describing them instead as constantly shifting border-zones, fundamentally contextual and perspectival:

> Above our real things the corresponding sky drifts toward the
>   edge of the
>   dark [. . .] as the sunset, claiming the horizon, binds it (by
> whatever is to come, whatever to continue) to the West.
> It is faced by an unbacked bench.
> The West?
> It is met with perception.
> Set with appreciation.
> And I am one
> Until I'm placed in the objective sense – am I to say 'prepared'?
>   – a person to turn sky around sun.
> An enclosure?
> Knowledge?
> [. . .] Still, I would get rid of *I* if I could, I said, I did, I went.[51]

The horizon offered in this extract is both image and imagery. In the mode of Heidegger, who was preoccupied with rediscovering pre-Socratic thinking and with hermeneutical horizons of meaning, especially in *Being and Time*, and also of Gadamer, who claimed that all understanding takes place within a certain 'horizon' that is historically conditioned, partial, perspectival and situated in language, Hejinian discerns knowledge to be a series of borders or horizons that we claim for ourselves, perceptions of which can become frozen in time. Such borders include, for example, the era of Socrates and Aristotle, which gave rise to logic and ratiocentric thought and the Age of 'the so-called Enlightenment'[52] as Hejinian describes it:

> [T]he moment when the West distinguished itself from the rest, is often said to have occurred between 500 and 399 B.C., in the century of Socrates, the period that defined and established the concept that fundamental laws might be discovered and incontrovertible logic be constructed for governing philosophy, science, and the social state.
> [. . .]
> But in considering contemporary experience, and particularly contemporary notions of what and how we know [. . .] an attempt to observe the West should be equally attentive to the fundamental redefinition and reevaluation of the rules of knowing . . .[53]

In 'La Faustienne', in particular, Hejinian investigates the gendered implications of traditional notions of knowledge and selfhood as complete and self-identical entities. Whilst acknowledging 'a certain heroic quality to the Faust figure'[54] – the quintessence of one whose insatiable desire for the acquisition and accumulation of knowledge proves his undoing – Hejinian decides that its motivation is 'so compromised that is seems to be an ultimately irrelevant heroism – misbegotten and probably contemptible'.[55]

Her essay charts the story of the real-life Faust, whose tragedy has become world-famous, but whose real value, for Hejinian, lies in its representativeness of 'the history of plunder and exploitation that Western knowledge-seekers have left behind them'.[56] The explorer, 'bachelor', 'scholar', 'scientist and doctor', 'consumed by love of knowledge which is transmuted into an overwhelming desire to know "everything"' is a familiar figure according to Hejinian.[57] He is responsible both for ransacking the already-occupied American continent, and simultaneously figuring such territory in terms of an unspoilt female othering: virgin, Paradise, mother, Eve, and so on – that 'kingdom, safeliest when with one man mann'd', according to John Donne's famous poem, 'To His Mistress Going to Bed'. Hejinian:

> Throughout the literature of the frontier, the intrepid Faustian discovers a *virgin landscape* and penetrates its wilderness [. . .] the unknown is imagined as an animate (though supine) other and she is female. The female element in this trope, then, is not the knower but the site of knowledge, its object and embodiment – that which is to be known.[58]

The linguistic trick goes both ways of course. Otherness, Hejinian explains, has tended to be personified as female; females as other. Thus, knowledge and the unknown have been sexualized and, the implication is, the need to contain woman, upheld. As Hejinian puts it: 'The erotic site is, then, a secret site – and it is, too, a threatening one, since it is also a source of power [. . .] Sexuality becomes the site of questions about what can and cannot be known.'[59]

Instead, she champions a model of knowledge represented by Scheherazade, a figure with 'creative and redemptive power'[60] closely aligned with the productive, literary imagination. After reading Sir Richard Burton's 1886 translation of *The Arabian Nights*,[61] Hejinian tells us, she realized she had found La Faustienne.

Her explicit gendering of these different models of knowledge is fascinating in the context of her own position as a female writer of Language poetry – one who both problematized the dominance of the individual in literary and political contexts, whilst understanding the importance of the subjective and personal. 'La Faustienne' appears to be Hejinian's attempt to grapple explicitly with such feminist dilemmas in the semi-mythologized, semi-historical space afforded her by the figures Faust and Scheherazade, as well as the neutralized realm, as she sees it, of night. Hejinian's questioning in these two essays of 'the dualism that is the basis for much of our Western thinking'[62] leads to her search for and discovery of a place where such binary thinking can be complicated – her 'night work':

The Proposition

> [M]y interest is in the processes of assimilation and assessment that take place in the figurative dark and silence of night, where opposites as such can't exist because they always coexist. I have wanted to write in the dark, so to speak, when the mind must accept the world it witnesses by day and out of all data assemble meaning. The writing would do so – assemble (a Faustian project) and in its way *make* knowledge (the work of La Faustienne).[63]

Here at night when her mind is less intentional or motivated and more open, to dreams and the imagination, Hejinian allows her semi-consciousness to '*make* knowledge' rather than simply to assemble what it already knows.[64] In other words, Hejinian enacts a Faustienne dynamic:

> The bed is made of sentences which present themselves as what they are
> Some soft, some hardly logical, some broken off
> Sentences granting freedom to memories and sights
> Then is freedom about love?
> Bare, and clumsily impossible?
> Our tendernesses give us sentences about our mistakes
> Our sentiments go on as described
> [...]
>
> The bed shows with utter clarity how sentences in saying something make
> something
> Sentences in bed are not describers, they are instigators ...[65]

Such a 'poem', situated unexpectedly in the middle of her essay, traces Hejinian's interest in recounting and exploring things as 'they are': illogical ('hardly logical') erroneous ('our mistakes') and fragmentary ('broken off'), which the poet associates with 'freedom', and with 'love' – followed by a question mark, i.e., uncertainly.

The last couple of sentences in the extract also reflect her poetic method more generally: letting the language itself spark new ideas, lead to new beginnings, rather than employing words to fit exactly predefined meanings. The most important lesson the 'wise and subtle' Scheherazade teaches the King Shahryar, Hejinian notes, is 'that every man is at the call of Fate' rather than fully in control of it.[66] This is a highly significant moral for Hejinian and resonates in the context of her work as a whole, with its emphasis on epistemological uncertainty and vulnerability in the face of the otherness with which we are always already surrounded. As she puts it at the end of 'La Faustienne', in 'A Fable' dedicated to another female Language poet and feminist, Carla Harryman, 'Various women writers will take up the philosophical quest for uncertainty.'[67]

Notes

1. Lyn Hejinian, *Happily* (California: Post-Apollo Press, 2000), 5.
2. Lyn Hejinian, *The Language of Inquiry* (Berkeley: University of California Press, 2000), 328. (Hereafter: *Inquiry*.)
3. Hejinian has participated in an array of collaborations, translations and mixed-genre works since the mid-1970s, in San Francisco, Berkeley and New York City, and in Leningrad-St. Petersburg since the 1980s. For instance, with fellow Language poets Leslie Scalapino, Barrett Watten, Carla Harryman, Kit Robinson, Michael Davidson and Ron Silliman, musician John Zorn, painter Emile Clark and director Jacki Ochs. She has also translated the work of Russian writers Arkadii Dragomoshchenko and Ilya Kutik.
4. Hejinian, *Inquiry*, 38.
5. Ibid., 4.
6. Ann Vickery, *Leaving Lines of Gender: A Feminist Genealogy of Language Writing* (Hanover, NH: Wesleyan Press, 2000).
7. Nicky Marsh, 'Infidelity to an Impossible Task: Postmodernism, Feminism and Lyn Hejinian's My Life', *Feminist Review*, 74, 'Fiction and Theory: Crossing Boundaries' (2003), 70–80, 70.
8. Cf. Ron Silliman's 'The New Sentence', Bruce Andrews' 'Text and Context', Charles Bernstein's 'Artifice of Absorption' and Steve McCafferey's 'The Death of the Subject' for examples of some pretty grandiose, if rhetorical, claims.
9. Her most well-known work, the prose poem *My Life*, has autobiographical elements, though it is far from being

'autobiography' as most people would understand the term. Lisa Samuels has usefully described it as 'autography', and points to its having been 'doubly *motivated* – by the personal and the literary – in a kind of arithmetics of autobiography'. Samuels, 'Eight Justifications for Canonizing Lyn Hejinian's *My Life*': http://epc.buffalo.edu/authors/samuels/mylife.html#1
10. 'Being-with' (*Mitsein*) is a Heideggerian formulation from the fourth chapter of his *Being and Time*, transl. John Macquarrie and Edward Robinson (Oxford: Blackwell, 1962). 'La Faustienne' is Hejinian's feminist take on the Faustian quest for knowledge – as explicated in this essay.
11. Hejinian, *Inquiry*, 70–1.
12. Emily Critchley, 'Dilemmatic Boundaries: Constructing a Poetics of Thinking', *Intercapillary/Space* (online, November 2006) and '[D]oubts, Complications and Distractions: Rethinking the Role of Women in Language Poetry', *Hot Gun! Journal*, #1, ed. Josh Stanley (summer 2009), 29–49.
13. Lyn Hejinian, *My Life in the Nineties* (New York: Shark Books, 2003), 67.
14. Hejinian: 'Poetry [. . .] is fundamentally an epistemological project [. . . But] the nature of knowing [. . .] is circumstantially embedded', *Inquiry*, 296.
15. Ibid.
16. See Hejinian's essay of that name, ibid., 232–67.
17. Ibid., 2.
18. Ibid., 365.
19. Ibid., 356.
20. Ibid., 365.
21. Ibid., 103.
22. Ibid., 351.
23. Lyn Hejinian, *Slowly* (California: Tuumba Press, 2002), 37.
24. Hejinian, *My Life* (Los Angeles, CA: Sun & Moon Press, 1987), 64.
25. Hejinian, *Inquiry*, 1.
26. Ibid., 340.
27. Cited by Hejinian, ibid., 347.
28. Ibid., 3.
29. Ibid., 269.
30. Hejinian, *Inquiry*, 351.
31. 'When man is capable of being in uncertainties, mysteries, doubts without any irritable reaching after fact and reason.'

Keats' letter to George and Thomas Keats dated Sunday, 21 December 1817. Nathan Scott notes that negative capability has been compared to Heidegger's concept of 'Gelassenheit': 'the spirit of disponibilité before What-Is which permits us simply to let things be in whatever may be their uncertainty and their mystery'. *Negative Capability: Studies in the New Literature and the Religious Situation* (New Haven, CT and London: Yale University Press, 1971).
32. Hejinian, *Inquiry*, 38.
33. Ibid., 332. Nicholls reads Oppen through the phenomenology of Emmanuel Levinas, whose notion of 'sincerity' had significant impact on the Objectivist poets.
34. Ibid.
35. Ibid., 337–54.
36. Exponents of aspects of 'virtue theory' include Gilligan and Nussbaum, the latter of whose *Love's Knowledge* (Oxford University Press, 1992) sees literature as a way of testing moral theory to see if it 'works'.
37. Hejinian, *Inquiry*, 2.
38. Ibid., 4.
39. Ibid., 250.
40. Ibid., 209–31.
41. Ibid., 211–12.
42. Ibid., 215.
43. Ibid., 209.
44. Ibid., 212. Cf. Heidegger's *Being and Time*, § 1.
45. Lyn Hejinian, *Oxota: A Short Russian Novel* (Massachusetts: The Figures, 1991).
46. Hejinian, *Inquiry*, 209–10.
47. Ibid., 199.
48. Lyn Hejinian, *A Border Comedy* (New York: Granary Books, 2001).
49. Lyn Hejinian, *The Cold of Poetry* (Los Angeles, CA: Sun and Moon Press, 2000).
50. Lyn Hejinian, *The Cell* (Los Angeles, CA: Sun and Moon Press, 1992).
51. Ibid., 212.
52. Hejinian, *Inquiry*, 233.
53. Ibid., 214.
54. Ibid., 233.
55. Ibid.

56. Ibid., 236–7.
57. Ibid., 237.
58. Ibid., 240.
59. Hejinian, *Inquiry*, 247.
60. Ibid.
61. Richard Burton, *Arabian Nights: Tales from a Thousand and One Nights* (New York: Modern Library, 2001).
62. I.e., man with mind, woman with matter. Ibid., 249. Cf. Hélène Cixous' 'Sorties: Out and Out: Attacks/WaysOut/Forays' for a deconstruction of this and other culturally assimilated binaries. *The Newly Born Woman*, transl. Betsy Wing (University of Minnesota Press: Minneapolis, 1986), 63–132.
63. Hejinian, *Inquiry*, 250.
64. Ibid.
65. Ibid., 250–1.
66. Ibid., 255.
67. Ibid., 261.

Crossing Improvised Boundaries: Personhood, Poetry, Estrangement
Jacob Edmond

Viktor Shklovsky's concept of estrangement (*ostranenie*) has attracted many avant-garde groups, but perhaps none more so than the Language writers. Among the Language writers, this theory of poetic estrangement finds no better expression than in the work of Lyn Hejinian. Like Shklovsky, Hejinian extends her poetics of estrangement beyond the textual, connecting the radical artifice of poetic language with the act of seeing the world anew and the estranging effect of Russia itself: the autonomous poetics of the word as such ("form made difficult") with the renewal of perception in everyday life.

According to Hejinian, "Sensation of the world and a counter to pessimism are what Language writers, when first encountering Shklovsky in the 1970s, found in his work."[1] It was in the mid-1970s that Barrett Watten and Ron Silliman, two members of the then-nascent Language poetry group, introduced her to Viktor Erlich's *Russian Formalism*, a book she describes as making an "enormous impact" on the Language poets at that time; of the Formalists, Shklovsky exerted the greatest influence on the group's "sense of literary style and strategies."[2] Shklovsky and Russian Formalism provided Hejinian and other Language poets with a method that emphasized poetic "technique" over the "subjective aesthetic approach" based on "values from psychology or biography." They also supplied the model for, in Hejinian's words, the "utopian project" of Language poetry: to create an artistic community in which theory and practice went hand in hand.[3]

Then, in 1983, Hejinian traveled to the USSR, the "home" of estrangement and, as fellow Language poet Michael Davidson puts it, the "fount" for Language poetry theory.[4] There, she established a friendship with the Russophone Ukrainian poet Arkadii Dragomoshchenko, initiating an intense personal and artistic engagement with the USSR and Russian and other Russia-based writers, which involved Hejinian learning Russian, making extensive and frequent trips to the Soviet Union, and translating the work of Dragomoshchenko and a number of other contemporary Russian-language poets.[5]

Hejinian's approximately eight-year period of close engagement with the USSR exemplifies how literary practice and theory are shaped from the outset by cross-cultural encounters. Hejinian tended to conflate the many peoples and lands of the USSR with "Russia" and "Russian." I largely follow her usage here but with full recognition that it is deeply problematic—see the essay's "Afterword." Her encounter with the USSR led her not only to explore the linguistic possibilities of translation but also to conflate estrangement in art and life.[6] Partly through her developing poetics of the "person," she came to link three kinds of estrangement: poetic estrangement, the estranging effect of her "Russian" experience, and estrangement as the basis for a community that would unite USSR and US writers. Entwining her poetics of the person with her poetic and personal engagement with the USSR, Hejinian's crosscultural encounter demonstrates that a theoretical term like "estrangement" is neither a free-floating concept of transnational Modernism, nor yet localized. Its various meanings emerge out of border-transcending visions and encounters among different places, times, and persons. So conceived, literary estrangement cannot easily be detached from everyday experiences of strangeness, nor can it be separated from the collective cross-cultural readings—such as those involved in the Cold War binaries of East and West, Russianness and Americanness—that shape those experiences.

The Person

Avant-garde artists such as Hejinian were drawn to Shklovsky's theory of art by the internal contradictions within its essential term, "estrangement." These are immediately apparent in the essay "Art as Device," where Shklovsky makes the famous statement: "in order to return sensation to life, to feel things, in order to make the stone stony, there exists that which is called art. The purpose of art is to impart a sensation of a thing as vision and not as recognition; the device of art is the device of 'estrangement.'" Shklovsky immediately adds, however, that the "device of art" involves not only returning "sensation to life" but also "the device of form made difficult (*zatrudnennaia forma*), which heightens the difficulty and length of perception, for the perceptual process in art is autonomous and should be prolonged."[7] Here the conception of poetic language as autonomous language that draws attention to words as such is combined with the view that poetic language is "expected to de-automatize and 'make strange' not only language but also the objects referred to."[8] Shklovsky's emphasis on perception contrasted with that of some other Formalists, such as Roman Jakobson.[9] Indeed, Shklovsky conflates two conceptions of poetic language, apparently without noticing, let alone acknowledging it: "If the process of perception becomes an end in itself through the difficulty of form, we perceive the object less, not more; if estrangement determines the definition of art, the process of perception is imperceptible, and we see the object instead, as if for the first time."[10] Shklovsky's famous passage from "Art as Device," then, proposes the "radical artifice" of the autonomous word as the basis of poetic language, but simultaneously argues that poetic language, through the device of estrangement, can also renew our perception of the world and can thus oppose the dreaded habituation, or "automatization," of language and perception that threatens to destroy any real experience of life.[11]

Shklovsky's conflation of "form made difficult" with the device of estranging the "real" world outside automatized experience has had an enduring appeal to avant-garde artists such as Hejinian, who wish to combine radical formal experimentation with the transformation of everyday life, because it "harbors the romantic and avantgarde dream of a reverse mimesis: everyday life can be redeemed if it imitates art, not the other way around. So the device of estrangement could both define and defy the autonomy of art." Moreover, estrangement, as Shklovsky conceived of it, was a peculiarly Russian concept, because for him it was only in Russia that the estrangement of everyday life could truly be realized. Russia offered the "imagined community of fellow intellectuals" necessary for this utopian goal, just as that same community provided the model for the utopian project of the Language poets.[12]

Following Shklovsky, Hejinian links estrangement in art and life, or what she refers to as "literary praxis" and "social materiality," terms that parallel fellow Language writer Watten's key theoretical concepts "material text" and "social poetics."[13] Hejinian develops her own distinct, though related, view of this relationship over the course of the 1980s and 1990s. She elaborates Shklovsky's original emphasis on perception through her key terms "experience," the "person," and "description," even as she opposes traditional preconceptions about lyric poetry that are sometimes associated with these terms.

Hejinian's statements about her poetry express the two apparently contradictory conceptions of poetic language in Shklovsky's work, but in her poetics these conceptions are combined through her key term "experience." In defining her poetics, Hejinian consciously echoes Shklovsky's famous statement in "Art as Device": "The function of art is to restore palpability to the world which habit and familiarity otherwise obscure; its task is to restore the liveliness to life. Thus it must make the familiar remarkable, noticeable again; it must render the familiar *unfamiliar*."[14] Here, the poetic function of estrangement is to renew perception. In the same essay, Hejinian also echoingly defines estrangement as all those effects that draw attention to the language itself, through "'roughening,' dissonances, impediments, etc."[15] Elsewhere, however, she describes these literary techniques not simply as drawing attention to language but as Shklovsky's "set of devices intended to restore palpability to things."[16] Like Shklovsky, she thus conflates these two forms of estrangement, so that the literary device of form made difficult operates "to alert us to the existence of life and give us the experience of experiencing."[17] But this goes further than Shklovsky, in that the estranging poetic text (a tautology for Hejinian) imparts an experience of the process of experiencing, or what she also calls a "consciousness of consciousness," because it draws attention to its own construction.[18] Through her concept of the "experience of experiencing," Hejinian provides a rationale for Shklovsky's original and unacknowledged conflation of two conceptions of poetic language. For Hejinian, the poetic text, through its impediments (its estranging, self-focused, "autonomous" devices), highlights the process of experiencing (experiential structure and contingency), even as it provides an experience that renews our perception of the world.

Hejinian thus gives "preeminence to experience," as "an extension of the poetics implied by Shklovsky's aphorism," one that she quotes twice in her book of essays: "In order to restore to us the perception of life, to make a stone stony, there exists that which we call art."[19] She rejects, however, the notion that a poetics of experience must "promote immediacy and disdain critique."[20] Rather, poetry affirms life by saying "this is happening" in context, "which is to say, in thought (in theory and with critique) and in history." Without thought, critique, and history, without a self-reflexive consideration of the basis of experience, "there is no sensation, no experience, no consciousness of living," only automatization, the loss of experience through the repetitions of everyday existence.[21]

Hejinian further develops her link between estrangement and experience through another central term in her poetics: the "person." In her essay "The Person and Description," first presented as a talk in 1988, during her period of intense involvement with the USSR, she argues, "It is on the improvised boundary between art and reality, between construction and experience, that the person (or my person) in writing exists."[22] In the same essay, Hejinian distinguishes the concepts "self" and "person." She notes that "each person is felt to be individualizing, different, unique." However, this uniqueness remains distinct from "essential selfhood": "Our individuality, in fact, is at odds with the concept of some core reality at the heart of our sense of being. The latter has tended to produce a banal description of the work of art as an expression uttered in the artist's 'own voice.'"[23]

Hejinian's poetic practice rejects the concept of "voice" and "all notions of the *self* as 'some core reality at the heart of our sense of being.'"[24] Many scholars have noted this rejection in her best-known poetic work, *My Life*, which is "a language field in which 'identity' is less a property of a given character than a fluid state that takes on varying shapes and that hence engages the reader to participate in its formation and deformation." In *My Life*, there is "a studied refusal to engage in introspection, a steady suspicion of Romantic self-consciousness."[25] Hejinian uses the estranging device of "radical parataxis" to avoid the impression of a singular, continuous self, taking "several complete narrative texts" and, as she puts it in *My Life*, breaking "them up into uncounted continuous and voluminous digressions." The effect is close "to what Gertrude Stein calls *Everybody's Autobiography*, in which the individual life is interwoven with language, perception, and social constructs in such a way that one cannot delineate where 'Lyn Hejinian' leaves off and the world begins."[26] In *My Life* "personal experiences" are transformed into "linguistic encounters" whose generalities all Americans might inhabit.[27] The self is dissolved as "my life" becomes anybody's life in language.

Yet the "I" continues to play a role in Hejinian's work, preserving a sense of individuality rather than merely linguistic play or inhabitability through a lyric mode that foregrounds the subject as a process rather than an identity, or in Hejinian's own terms, as a "person" rather than a "self," a distinction that she developed in the late 1980s, during and through her contact with Russia and Russia-based writers.[28] Hejinian rejects the focus on "the self of the English language, whose definition posits it as the essence of each single human being, the sole and constant point from which the human being can truthfully and originally speak."[29] She contrasts the English word "self" with the lack of an exact Russian equivalent, suggesting that notions of personhood in Russian are consequently more dynamic and less fixed than English selfhood. Although Hejinian's distinction between Russian and English may seem forced, given the strong sense of self in the Russian poetic tradition, it nevertheless allows her to develop a critical concept in her poetics.[30] Instead of the self, Hejinian envisions a dynamic entity she terms the "person": "the exercise of possibilities (including that of consciousness) amid conditions and occasions constitutes a person." This person is "a relationship rather than an essence," and "it is here that the epistemological nightmare of the solipsistic self breaks down, and the essentialist yearning after truth and origin can be discarded in favor of the experience of experience."[31] Hejinian associates a non-essentialist, dynamic personhood with the "experience of experience" and thus links the Russian language—which, in her view, lacks an exact equivalent for "self"—with Shklovsky's conception of poetic language as the language of estrangement. For Hejinian, estrangement imparts to the reader an "experience of experience," but this effect is also central to her concept of the person, which "consists of and is known by its descriptions of its own experiences."[32] Hejinian thus sees the "experience of experience" imparted through Russian estrangement as critical to her conception and poetic exploration of the person as "relationship rather than an essence."

Through her conceptions of experience and the person, Hejinian links her poetics of estrangement to the poetics of everyday life by introducing a third key term: "description." In her prefatory note to "The Person and Description," Hejinian writes of description as being "pivotal to the question of personhood and hence to everyday life": it occupies an intermediary zone between "art and reality" to create "a space through which a person might step."[33] In her essay "Strangeness," Hejinian defines "description" as a response to the world not already shaped by everyday assumptions, presented "in the terms 'there it is,' 'there it is,' 'there it is,'" citing as examples the narratives of explorers and descriptions of dreams.[34] Description thus has a "marked tendency toward effecting isolation and displacement, that is toward objectifying all that's described and making it strange," a statement that alludes to Shklovsky's concept of estrangement.[35] Description here allows Hejinian to enact her dynamic conceptions of personhood and the "experience of experience" because, so defined, it refuses preconceived notions of self and world. It also links estrangement in art and life because, as her examples show, description for her explicitly relates estranging writing to encounters with strangeness in the world. Such description is

> "phenomenal" in the double sense of acknowledging the claims of both the facticity of experience and its strangeness. And this strangeness is the strangeness of some middle ground, where we are somehow caught between the generalizing, abstracting quality of language, on the one hand, and an engagement with the localized forms of a particular perceptual world, on the other.[36]

Hejinian's concept of description reflects the development of a "new sociality" in her work that seems at odds with the tendency of critics of Language writing, especially in the 1980s, "to focus almost exclusively on modes of self-reflexivity and on a subversion of conventional models of self."[37] Over the course of the 1980s and 1990s, "a decrease in fragmentation, and an increase in complete sentences and discernible narrative structures or gestures" clearly develops in the work of several Language writers, so that the "social variety of the writing is greater." This shift is evident between Hejinian's *Writing Is an Aid to Memory* (1978) and *Oxota: A Short Russian Novel* (1991), in which she most explicitly and extensively uses material from her experiences of the USSR and from Russophone literature and literary theory.[38] Yet this new sociality begins as early as *The Guard* (1984), in which Hejinian's first clear articulation of her poetics of the person coincides with her initial encounter with Russia.

Hejinian theorized poetic estrangement as a way to affirm personhood, sociality, and community without essentializing identity. Her contact with Russia provided another way for her to oppose the strictures of essentialist, restrictive identity, while emphasizing sociality. First, by engaging with Russia, Hejinian escaped from the realm of US poetry, in which the typecasting of the Language poets and the attacks on their poetics in the 1980s evidenced the difficulties and restrictions of community identity, even an identity based on opposition to essential identity.[39] Second, Hejinian's engagement with Russia opposed the essentialist binary models of identity central to Cold War politics, such as Russian versus American and communist versus capitalist. Instead, she can be seen partly as living out what Watten, quoting William Carlos Williams, has described as the dream of a "wedding between Russia and the United States," a utopian vision based on the model of Shklovsky's community of intellectuals, the OPOYAZ.[40] This dream is evident in *Leningrad: American Writers in the Soviet Union* (1991), an account by Hejinian and fellow Language poets Michael Davidson, Ron Silliman, and Barrett Watten of their 1989 visit to Leningrad to attend the international conference "Language—Consciousness—Society." In providing the common ground on which to unite Russian and US writers, estrangement came to stand for the idealized vision of an artistic community that would bridge the Cold War divide, just as Hejinian identified estrangement as enabling a middle ground between life and art. A US poet using utopian Russian theory could dream of reconciling both oppositions.[41]

Hejinian's Russian estrangement became a key point of contact between the material text and the social poetics of everyday life, linking art to life through the figure of the person. The encounter with Russia reinforced her sense of a relation between existential and poetic estrangement: it drew her attention to the extraordinary strangeness and contingencies of being a person and encouraged her to conflate this strangeness with the estranging qualities that she saw as essential to poetic language. Russia became a key site for poetic and existential exploration as she developed her theory of estrangement. She found that the experience of being in a radically different cultural context alerted her to the contingencies of personhood, just as the estranging effects of poetry highlighted the contingencies of description in language. Hejinian thus came to conflate poetic estrangement not only with the utopian vision of uniting Russia and the United States but also with the estrangement produced by her experience of Russia itself.

Encounters

When Hejinian first traveled to the Soviet Union in June 1983, she had been concerned for some time about the direction taken by her circle of writers. Her letters, journals, and the texts of several talks show that, prior to her trip, she was already thinking about subjectivity and the mediation of experience as critical issues for investigation, which she felt were undervalued in the Language poetry community.[42] At this time, however, Hejinian still expressed her belief in the primacy of artistic devices and words as such in poetry.[43] Her trip to Russia seems to have encouraged her to relate poetry and poetic estrangement more directly to social and existential questions of consciousness and experience, issues that coincided or found resonance with those current in Russia's unofficial writing community.

Hejinian's first trip to Russia was very brief, but her correspondence with poets and translators after that trip may have made her look at her own work in a new way, because it forced her to explain her poetics to writers who were not necessarily familiar with her approach to writing or its underlying assumptions. In Leningrad, she left behind several books of poetry, one of which included her poem "The Altitudes." The poet Vladimir Kucheriavkin began translating "The Altitudes" immediately after Hejinian left. He sent her questions about the poem, which he clearly found somewhat bewildering.[44] In response, Hejinian explained the estranging impediments of her poetic language by linking these techniques with existential estrangement, describing her poem as "an autobiography . . . whose subject is the life of the mind."[45]

The influence of Hejinian's experience of Russia on the link she developed between poetic and existential estrangement becomes more evident in her long poem *The Guard*, begun before her first trip to Russia and completed in 1984. The poem represented a new stage in her attempt to combine linguistic materiality with a socially located poetics of the person.[46] Hejinian herself draws a connection between her experience of existential estrangement in Russia and her use of poetic estrangement in *The Guard*: the poem resulted not only from the "disorientation and longing" that she experienced through her encounter with Russia and the Russian language, but from a "similar disorientation and longing" that informed much of her writing.[47]

Her increasing interest in the phenomenology of experience, already evident in her comment to Kucheriavkin, and a new interest in the strangeness of Russia are both evident in the poem. One clear Russian influence in *The Guard* is the use of Russian animal noises:

> But I tell you that cats "say" *mya-ew, mya-ew*
> dogs *gav-gav*, trains *sheex-sheex-sheekh*
> (while whistling *ta-tooo*), roosters cry
> *coo-caw-reh-coo*, frogs croak *kva-kva*, birds
> in a flock sing *fyou-eet*, except ravens
>
> which prefer *karr-karr*, and the ducks quack *kra*
> bells ring *bom-bomm*, and pigs grunt *hryou-hryou*[48]

The use of Russian animal noises highlights the arbitrary nature of onomatopoeic words. This conventionality is only revealed in the quoted passage when translation is compared to transliteration. Hejinian writes about this effect in section 44 of *My Life*, which corresponds to the forty-fourth year of her life (1984–5), the time just after she had written *The Guard*: "But any translator will complain, woof is translation and gav transliteration."[49] The plain everyday English "woof, woof" also becomes strange when compared to the bark of a dog, because it is shown to be not a transliteration of the dog's bark, but a translation from animal sound into language, which is conventionalized and uses a limited number of phonemes. Through a Shklovskian device of poetic estrangement, the passage draws attention to its linguistic materiality, while also making the reader attend to the phenomenal reality of that which it describes—or as Shklovsky might have said, it renews the barkness of the dog's bark. This passage from *The Guard* thus establishes a direct link between Hejinian's experience of Russia and Russian and her poetics of estrangement.

Hejinian's second trip to Russia in May through June 1985 had an even greater impact on her developing linkage between estrangement in art and life. On May 28, 1985 in Leningrad, Hejinian gave a talk on contemporary US poetry, in which she discussed Language writing and talked about her own work, focusing on *The Guard*. Her talk emphasized her interest in writing lyric poetry that was a site for consciousness and that addressed the lyric problems of self-expression and mediation. In relation to *The Guard*, she noted that "the question of mediation, of poetic language as mediation, is an old problem with lyric poetry—the lament in lyric poetry of the poet unable to say, unable to capture in words, his or her desire to say whatever it is he or she wants to say."[50] Here one sees Hejinian seeking to relate the resistance or impediments of poetic estrangement, which emphasize the mediating role of language, to questions of experience and its expression in language.

During her 1985 trip, Hejinian began to recognize that Russia played a crucial role in her exploration of such relationships. Soon after leaving Russia, she wrote in her journal:

> In Russia I felt the inadequacy of my description . . . of my writing—the subject and the metaphysics of my project.

In our circle, discussion is more technical than metaphysical, and I suspect us of being embarrassed by our potential metaphysics ... One element of my attachment to Arkadii—my need for him, or at least, my *use* for him (he too uses me, and this reciprocal necessity is part of the amorous dynamic that is characteristic of our imagination of each other)—involves a displacement—or replacement, rather, of the emotional center of my work, *away* from the Language School condition.

Hejinian then attempted to list the contents of her work in her journal. First on that list was "a phenomenology of consciousness: perception, psychology, reality," which addressed "the position of a person in the real world." This phenomenology was to be "located within the context of *poetic* language," and language was to become "the site of a *poetry of consciousness*."[51] Hejinian thus interrelates the poetics of estrangement with a poetics of phenomenology and consciousness, insisting that mediation and the strangeness to which it gives rise are necessary parts of the experience of being a person in the world, or what she would later call her experience of being a person as a "relationship rather than an essence."[52]

Her heightened interest in this interpolation arose in two ways from her experience of Russia. The first was simply the estranging effect that Russia itself had on Hejinian. Her list of the contents of her work ends with the following comment: "For days at a time in Russia I was not conscious of being conscious."[53] The foreignness of everyday Russia unsettled both her assumptions as a person and her experience of the world, thus heightening her awareness of the contingencies involved.

Second, the discussion of what Hejinian referred to as "meaning"—and what she had missed within her own group of poets in the United States—was central to her literary conversations in Russia and also had an impact on her work. In a letter to the poet Ilya Kutik, she describes the importance of a particular conversation:

The Proposition

> By the way, did you know that you yourself had a certain influence on my writing, beginning in 1985? In our circle here we often talked about writing, and sometimes about what we were working on at the time, but usually our discussions were technical, about devices rather than "meanings." ... Then in Moscow, in 1985, when we were sitting at a table ... we began talking about poetry, but at the level of "meaning"— which I found strangely exhilarating and liberating— while it was clear that we all assumed that poetic language is, as you say, the object-subject of thinking, of inquiring, of such "meaning." In any case, that conversation gave me the courage and context for clarifying my writing and my intentions. Or, to put it another way, I began to insist on acknowledging not just *how* there is writing, but also *why* there is writing.[54]

This letter refers specifically to Kutik's statement that "in his poetry he was asking the question, 'Do objects die?'"[55] Kutik thus began with the existential status of objects in the world, rather than with a question of poetic technique, in contrast to the emphasis on technique and its priority to meaning that Hejinian noted within her own circle. By paying greater attention to objects in the phenomenal world, Hejinian came, like Shklovsky, to articulate the relationship between the techniques of estrangement and the very things observed and experienced. By allowing meaning, experience, or abstract ideas to come before their formal realization, she could develop further her phenomenology of description and strangeness. Moreover, Kutik's question resonated with the link that Hejinian was developing between poetic estrangement and the disorienting loss of objects that characterized her experience of Russia.

Hejinian immediately started building on what she had gained from her trip to Russia. In June 1985, the same month she returned to the United States, she attended the New Poetics Colloquium at the Kootenay School of Writing in Vancouver. There she presented a talk on *The Guard*, titled "Language and 'Paradise.'"[56] In a letter, she described her talk as "broaching various metaphysical concerns à la discussions in Moscow and Leningrad."[57]

At the colloquium, Hejinian also read from her unfinished poem "The Person," the very title of which emphasizes Hejinian's increasing interest in writing about the lyric problem of personhood. "The Person" would later provide the inspiration and materials for Hejinian's essay "The Person and Description," which, as seen above, identifies the "person" as a key middle term between everyday life and the estranging effects of art. In September 1985, after her second trip to Russia, she worked on the final three sections of "The Person." These sections are strikingly lyrical and show her interest in direct confrontation with metaphysical and epistemological issues related to her concept of personhood: the last section begins with the line "Realism is an unimaginable ballad" and includes the word NATURE twice in capital letters. In this section, Hejinian investigates the phenomenological relationship of a person to the world and the way a person is simultaneously a part of that world:

> Described, the corresponding sky
> in circumstantial detail goes up
> as if having yielded—blue
> seems to yield to our gaze—
> having as its object something unknown but conscious
> Below the brain are overt gates[58]

Hejinian here cites the collaborative poetic project The Corresponding Sky that she and Dragomoshchenko had recently embarked upon. The name most obviously referred to the extensive correspondence between the two poets that formed such an important part of their relationship. It was, however, also suggestive of the relationship between words and things, which was at the heart of the project. Both poets set out to write works that explored the phenomenology of perception and description.[59] Hejinian's part of the project was "The Person," while Dragomoshchenko produced a large number of poems that he published under the title *Nebo sootvetstvii* (*Sky of Correspondences*). Both poets focused on description in these poems. In the quoted passage, Hejinian undermines the common association of "circumstantial" with something anecdotal, and not generally valid, by suggesting that, far from being imprecise, the description of "the corresponding sky" is detailed. Further, "circumstantial" implies being located in time, which human consciousness always is.

The "corresponding sky" also sets up a link between things: not only between the person and nature but also between one person and another. Hejinian describes the processes of perception and description as sensuous. Object and subject are animated: "blue / seems to yield to our gaze." The object of the gaze is "unknown but / conscious," not only because what is out there in the world is perceived only through the conscious mind of the observer but, less obviously, because being conscious entails the registration of what is unknown, or strange. The world yields to the gaze, but the gaze must also yield to the strangeness and estranging effects of the world. Hejinian thus presents phenomenal experience as an interactive process among mind, eye, and world in which existential estrangement plays a central role. The final line also suggests interaction. The "overt gates" imply that the interaction is sexual, although the phrase could also stand for oral communication through the gate of the mouth, or, perhaps most clearly, of the eyes. The line makes the normal strange by describing eyes, mouth, or sexual organs as "overt gates." Strange in itself, "gates" is made stranger by the use of "overt" instead of "open." "Overt" in turn opens up a connection with the idea of making something visible implied by "yields to our gaze." This estranging use of "gates" draws attention to the bodily nature of consciousness, the brain, and the bodily organs implied by the word. But significantly, this bodily aspect of the person (in the poem's title) is a portal, not an essence. That person consists in a dynamic process of interaction between subject and object: the "gates" of perception and the mediation of language highlighted by the poem's estranging devices.

Notwithstanding her continued avoidance of direct, unmediated self-expression, Hejinian confronts the phenomenal nature of being a person in *The Guard* and "The Person" more directly than in her earlier writing. Even her apparently more personal work *My Life*, first published in 1980, focuses more on the language that makes up a life, than it does on the phenomenology of being a person. Hejinian's increasing tendency to link estrangement to her notion of the person can be attributed at least partly to her contact with Russia.

Russia became, however, more than just an aesthetic pivot for Hejinian. Her intensive involvement with Russia was motivated by her deep personal attraction based in part on a certain aesthetic quality of estrangement that she found in everyday life there. After a visit in 1987, she wrote to Michael Molnar about her "romance" with Russia: "I was thinking that surely Russia isn't magical. That is, I was forgetting. It is—I'm mystified, but it is. I had moments when I felt completely isolated, and thought maybe I was losing personality and would become no one. . . . [But then] I began speaking Russian . . . It is amazing how direct the link between personality (or person) and language is."[60] Hejinian here locates her romance with Russia in her experience of the loss and then transformation of self: the estranging effect of being unable to speak the local language and, as her fluency increased, of being translated into a Russian person. She was attracted by the similarities between this loss of self in Russia and the loss of essential selfhood that she sought to enact in her poetry.

Afterword

Afterword in the sense that these words conclude the essay, but also afterword in the sense that I write these words almost two decades after I initially drafted the essay that I present here in a new iteration.

Initially I thought merely to republish what I had first written, but on reading over it twenty years later I found it impossible not to attempt a few revisions. Like Hejinian's (or my) personhood, an essay is a constant improvisation whose meaning will change even when the words stay the same. So I found with one of this essay's key words: *Russia* and its derivatives *Russian* and *Russianness*.

The Proposition

I can see now that I should not have unproblematically referred to Dragomoshchenko as a *Russian* poet. Not only does he bear a Ukrainian surname, but he was born in Potsdam (where his father was stationed with the occupying Soviet forces) and grew up in Vinnitsa in Ukraine, where he spoke Ukrainian as a first language.[61] As Hejinian noted in her moving tribute to Dragomoshchenko after his death in 2012, he wrote with passion about the many languages he heard on the streets of Vinnitsa as a child and about the multilingual, multi-ethnic, and multi-faith history of his childhood town.[62] It is true that he wrote in Russian, lived most of his adult life in St Petersburg, and was (until recently at least) widely referred to as a Russian poet. That adjective now, however, seems deeply problematic in its erasure of the fact that he "spent his childhood and youth in Vinnitsa, a city which, like hundreds of other Ukrainian cities, is now being bombed by the armed forces of the Russian Federation." In a statement beginning with this fact, the Arkadii Dragomoshchenko Prize was indefinitely suspended in 2022 as an act of solidarity with the poets of Ukraine and in recognition that "the normalization of cultural life in Russia today is impossible."[63]

I offer my revisions and this afterword not only in similar solidarity with those suffering under Russian military bombardment but also because to revise the essay in this way is to further cross and unsettle the deceptively neat boundaries of personal and national identity that my account of Hejinian's "Russian estrangement" both relies on and seeks to question. I argued twenty years ago that Hejinian's approach to Russia and Russianness was somewhat romanticized, exoticized, and oversimplified, but that point appears more obvious today when those terms—which, like American and Americanness, always carried a history and present of imperialism—weigh so much more heavily.

And yet there remains much to learn from Hejinian's self-questioning poetics of improvised boundaries—her refusal to treat language as isolated from reality, whether everyday or geopolitical, and her simultaneous estranging rejection of the oversimplified accounts of identity that feed nationalism, xenophobia, and imperialism. An earlier version of this essay appeared in my first book, *A Common Strangeness*, which attempts to tell the story of missed opportunities, glimpsed in poetry, for a world less locked in the binary oppositions that crumbled all too briefly at the end of the Cold War only to re-emerge with vigour in new (and depressingly old) forms. If Hejinian's encounter with the USSR is born partly out of the naivety of a traveler seeking to traverse, but nevertheless caught within, the strict boundaries of Cold War opposition, of Russian and US imperialism, then that encounter, at a personal and poetic level, also contains lessons for other ways of imagining relation and personhood, other ways of being and writing in the world.

Notes

1. Hejinian, Afterword, 105.
2. Hejinian, "Roughly Stapled."
3. Watten, *Total Syntax*, 1; Hejinian, "Roughly Stapled."
4. Michael Davidson, conversation with the author, August 26, 2003.
5. Hejinian's initial trip to Russia is documented in Hejinian, notebook, June 7–15, 1983, Lyn Hejinian Papers, box 47, folder 1. Correspondence and documents from these papers show that she made at least six subsequent trips to Russia: in 1985, 1987, 1989 (twice), 1990, and 1991.
6. On her poetics of translation, see Janecek, "Lin Khedzhinian"; Edmond, "Meaning Alliance."
7. Shklovsky, "Iskusstvo," 13. While I draw freely on translations by Lemon and Reis and by Sher, I have chosen to translate this passage myself in the interests of literalness and the preservation of ambiguities. Shklovsky, "Art as Technique," 12; Shklovsky, *Theory of Prose*, 6.
8. Matejka, "Formal Method," 285.
9. Erlich, *Russian Formalism*, 154.
10. Todorov, "Three Conceptions," 139.
11. Perloff, *Radical Artifice*. On estrangement as a device of mediation between art and life, see Steiner, *Russian Formalism*;

Striedter, *Literary Structure*. Jameson also discusses what he sees as the "profound ambiguity" in Shklovsky's theory of poetic language, an ambiguity he identifies primarily in the tension between estrangement in content and form, the latter implying an autonomous aesthetic. Jameson, *Prison-House of Language*, 75–9.
12. Boym, "Estrangement as a Lifestyle," 515, 518.
13. Hejinian, *Language of Inquiry*, 161; Watten, *Constructivist Moment*.
14. Hejinian, *Language of Inquiry*, 301 (emphasis in the original).
15. Hejinian, *Language of Inquiry*, 301.
16. Hejinian, *Language of Inquiry*, 344.
17. Hejinian, *Language of Inquiry*, 301.
18. Hejinian, *Language of Inquiry*, 144, 344. Variations on these expressions, central to her definition of poetry, recur throughout Hejinian's essays. In *Language of Inquiry*, see, for example, "experiencing of experience" (3); "consciousness of life" (8); "consciousness of perception" (67); "experience of experience" (203); "thinking of thinking" (300); "experiences of our perceptions" (315); "experiencing experience" and "consciousness of consciousness" (344); and "*experience* of our experience" (345).
19. Hejinian, *Language of Inquiry*, 344, 95, 343.
20. Hejinian, *Language of Inquiry*, 345.
21. Hejinian, *Language of Inquiry*, 345–6. Hejinian's extension of estrangement to historical context resembles that made by Tynianov and that involved in Jameson's critique of Shklovsky's theory. See Tynianov, "O literaturnoi evoliutsii"; Todorov, "Three Conceptions"; Jameson, *Prison-House of Language*.
22. Hejinian, *Language of Inquiry*, 207.
23. Hejinian, *Language of Inquiry*, 201.
24. Perloff, "How Russian Is It?," 193.
25. Perloff, "Sweet Aftertaste," 122, 126.
26. Dworkin, "Penelope Reworking the Twill," 69, 62.
27. Samuels, "Eight Justifications," 116, 111–13.
28. Writing of *The Cell* (1992), a work composed in the late 1980s, during Hejinian's period of contact with Russia, Altieri suggests that Hejinian "dissolves fixed identity while preserving a range of values like individuality and intimacy which have derived from now outmoded depth-psychology versions of selfhood." Altieri, "Lyn Hejinian," 149. She focuses on "the

subject's experience," even as she rejects dramatic climaxes "because the dramatic organization blinds the author to the most intimate features of repetition and change as life unfolds, and it greatly oversimplifies the play of voices that constitute self-consciousness within that unfolding." Altieri, "Lyn Hejinian," 150.
29. Hejinian, *Language of Inquiry*, 201–2.
30. Perloff, "How Russian Is It?," 193. Stephanie Sandler also discusses this contrast. See Sandler, "Arkadii Dragomoshchenko, Lyn Hejinian," 22–3.
31. Hejinian, *Language of Inquiry*, 202–3.
32. Fredman, "Lyn Hejinian's Inquiry," 63.
33. Hejinian, *Language of Inquiry*, 200.
34. Hejinian, *Language of Inquiry*, 158.
35. Hejinian, *Language of Inquiry*, 138; Shoptaw, "Hejinian Meditations," 60.
36. Nicholls, "Phenomenal Poetics," 243.
37. Nicholls, "Phenomenal Poetics," 241.
38. Perelman, "Polemic Greeting," 376.
39. Altieri argues that Language poetry both advocates a politics of identity and rejects identity. Altieri, "What Is Living." Watten also makes this point, while challenging the conclusions Altieri draws from it in some respects. Watten, *Constructivist Moment*, 116–18. For an account of one attack on Language poetry in the 1980s, see Sloan, "'Crude Mechanical Access.'"
40. Watten, *Constructivist Moment*, xviii.
41. Izenberg has addressed the social poetics of Language poetry partly in relation to their contact with Russia, identifying Language poetry's ethos of "collective life" with the collaborative book *Leningrad*. (On the poetics of collective voice in *Leningrad*, see also Silliman, "Task of the Collaborator.") Izenberg argues that the effect produced by Language poetry is one of "anaesthesis," rather than estrangement, suggesting that Language poetry texts such as *Leningrad* assert a universal human capacity to produce sentences. Izenberg, "Language Poetry," 135. Hejinian's poetics of estrangement suggests, however, that the sociality of her work is located precisely in the aesthetic, estranging quality of her poetry, a quality that Izenberg dismisses as largely irrelevant to Language poetry. For Hejinian, "aesthetic discovery is also social

discovery." Hejinian, *Language of Inquiry*, 170. Moreover, where Izenberg argues that Language poetry "is not oriented toward... perception," Hejinian insists, following Shklovsky, that the "function of art is to restore palpability to the world." Izenberg, "Language Poetry," 136; Hejinian, *Language of Inquiry*, 301. Far from emphasizing the universal everyday human capacity to produce language, therefore, Hejinian's poetics of estrangement stresses the extraordinary nature of poetic language.

42. For example, in a letter to Susan Bee and Charles Bernstein, Hejinian questioned why some Language poets refused to discuss subjectivity: "Why was the term subjectivity inadmissible, even as something to talk about? Self-expression is an obvious irrelevancy. But subjectivity?... What does it mean when one feels one 'doesn't have anything to say'? Who/what determines valid and relevant styles and topics of discourse? (This is the one that concerns me personally—and prompts my question about the topic subjectivity.)" Lyn Hejinian to Susan Bee and Charles Bernstein, February 13, 1983, Lyn Hejinian Papers, box 2, folder 10.
43. Lyn Hejinian to Ron Silliman, January 21, 1982, Lyn Hejinian Papers, box 7, folder 6.
44. Vladimir Kucheriavkin to Lyn Hejinian, [November] 1983, Lyn Hejinian Papers, box 5, folder 11.
45. Lyn Hejinian to Vladimir Kucheriavkin, November 7, 1983, Lyn Hejinian Papers, box 5, folder 11.
46. Nicholls, "Phenomenal Poetics"; Edmond, "Locating Global Resistance."
47. Hejinian, *Language of Inquiry*, 196.
48. Hejinian, *Guard*, 30.
49. Hejinian, *My Life*, 156.
50. Hejinian, talk on US poetry given in Leningrad, May 28, 1985, Lyn Hejinian Papers, box 53, folder 15, audiocassette.
51. Hejinian, notebook, August 24, 1984–July 1985, Lyn Hejinian Papers, box 47, folder 6, p. 90 (emphases in the original).
52. Hejinian, *Language of Inquiry*, 202.
53. Hejinian, notebook, August 24, 1984–July 1985, Lyn Hejinian Papers, box 47, folder 6, p. 91.
54. Lyn Hejinian to Ilya Kutik, June 8, 1990, Lyn Hejinian Papers, box 24, folder 9 (emphasis in the original).
55. Lyn Hejinian, email to the author, January 15, 2005.

56. This talk was published under the same title in Hejinian, *Language of Inquiry*, 59–82. In the preface to the published version, Hejinian herself notes the influence of her second trip to Russia on the essay and compares it to the influence of her first trip on *The Guard*. Hejinian, *Language of Inquiry*, 59.
57. Lyn Hejinian to Michael Molnar, September 6, 1985, Lyn Hejinian Papers, box 27, folder 7.
58. Hejinian, "Person," 179–80.
59. See Edmond, "Meaning Alliance."
60. Lyn Hejinian to Michael Molnar, June 8, 1987, Lyn Hejinian Papers, box 27, folder 8.
61. Pavlov, "Here and There," 169.
62. Hejinian, "Po tu storonu konechnosti."
63. "Premiia Arkadiia Dragomoshchenko."

Lyn Hejinian's "Allegorical Activism"

Jessica Fisher

> I come face to face with a still life, but it isn't even *still*; even *it* isn't still.
>
> Lyn Hejinian, *Tribunal*[1]
>
> A German goldsmith covered a bit of metal with cloth in the fourteenth century and gave humankind its first button. It was hard to know this as politics, because it plays like the work of one person, but nothing is isolated in history.
>
> Lyn Hejinian, *My Life*[2]

We live in the world, but also in language. This is the fact of our being. And from this (seemingly banal) fact stems the radical writing of Lyn Hejinian, a founding member of the Language movement and arguably our foremost poet-critic. For many of her readers, Hejinian has managed to alter what we think of as a life. Rather than made of Virginia Woolf's crystallized "moments of being," life for Hejinian is instead a form of *ongoingness*, marked by relation and contingency and formed through the play of language and of the imagination, as well as through historical forces. As she writes in the epigraph above, it's "hard to know this as politics, because it plays like the work of one person, but nothing is isolated in history."

Hejinian's revelrous, rebellious writing continually works against our sense of isolation. Her texts—which now number more than twenty-five volumes of poetry and critical prose, as well as numerous translations and collaborations—are maximally alive, responsive to an ever-evolving present in which the personal and the political are inextricably linked. This ongoing commitment to aesthetic and political resistance is why she remains, in her seventh decade, an avant-garde writer. "At the heart of avant-gardism," she explains, "is the belief that artistic practice should aim to produce not bodies of works but series of actions. It's for this reason that we can term avant-gardes movements rather than schools. They are activist."[3]

As is true in art, so too in politics, and even psychology. "Subjectivity is not an entity but a dynamic," as Hejinian explores in her masterwork *My Life*, a work of experimental autobiography first published in 1980. "There is no self undefiled by experience, no self unmediated by the perceptual situation; instead there is a world and the person is in it."[4] To pretend otherwise, she suggests in her most recent book of poems, *Tribunal*, is to be a tyrant:

> The tyrant closes the world tightly around himself, he is in the embrace of his own narcissism.
> With the melancholy of self-condemnation and a pen, I, also a tyrant, draw a wall.
> Stand, attend, account, shout.
> All ideas but no acts so no association, no activism, no theater.
> A tyrant proclaims that the future dreams of him, which only means that old age dreams of him.[5]

In this negative vision, which links authoritarianism with narcissism, the writer is figured as the self-enclosed "I" who, like the political tyrant, demands obedience and obeisance. Here we have everything that Hejinian is not. Instead, in each of her books she enacts the alternatives to such reification, creating dynamic and active spaces of perception and invention.

Hejinian's war on tyranny is not new. We see it in myriad ways throughout her earlier works, in her antilyricism, her "rejection of closure," and her revelation of language's slippages.[6] As is true in the work of Language writers more generally, there has always been a politics to her poetic forms. What *is* new in her most recent books is the explicit emphasis on political activism and the turn toward allegory as a gesture of what she calls "wild captioning." Both *Tribunal* and her recent prose work *Positions of the Sun* theorize and perform the radical pleasures of an immersive writing. Perhaps more importantly, they are both works of "allegorical activism, or of activist allegorizing, as an artistic and as a political practice . . . in the service of activating some of the creative potential in everyday life."[7]

Such motile work resists description. Indeed, often when critics write about her work, they lift from the poems' disjunctive atmospheres those moments that crystallize as aphoristic thought. But that doesn't give much of a sense of the effect of her writing, the way it works in and on the present. And since Hejinian wants to make "writing that is generative rather than directive," one would have to describe not what it says, but what it *does*.[8]

So, what does Hejinian's writing do? And how does she manage to bring her antiprivatization activism into aesthetic form? In many ways, *Positions of the Sun* carries forth the project of the now canonical *My Life*; the books share, as Hejinian notes, an interest in "chronological organization, paratactic structure, attention to the 'sentence' (as distinct from the 'line')."[9]

But while *My Life* unfolds in the past tense and carries along with it "memory[, which] provokes a ready pathos," *Positions* is committed to bringing forth a vision of collective life in the present.[10] The book begins with the sun's rising, and the illumination it brings. Not of the mind—of things.

> The sun is rising. Chuk-a-chuka-chuk, chuka-chuk, chuka-chuk. How we love it! The petals of the sun flare, waver, bend, spin. Someone sings. Light comes through a window, falls across a plate, illuminates the mottled surface of a shark's tooth, a small red pocketknife. Humans are forever creating new allegories out of things they find in the world. A feather, a paper flag on a stick, and an ivory chopstick are stuck beside an upright tulip in a jar.[11]

The sun moves as the mind does, over things, and becomes itself an allegory for the mind. "The sun moves relentlessly," she writes, "slowly but without caution; with each change of position, it withdraws its light from one thing and casts it onto the next, allegorizing and then de-allegorizing and then re-allegorizing again. Continuity is made, not found."[12]

In this allegory of her own practice, with its commitment to the "paratactic present"—in which perceptions arise one after the other, in a nonhierarchical unfolding—the anxieties that govern daily life momentarily give way.[13] Why? "Anxiety is an engine as well as a product of postmodern affect," Hejinian writes; it "renders synchronization (the bringing into pleasurable play of numerous facilities attentive to numerous experiences) impossible. It cuts humans off from the medium in which they live—present time."[14]

To counter this distraction, "the writer of everyday life" creates a "paratactically configured work [that] keeps first her and then our attention on immediate particulars in the present tense, since that is the tense of cognitive time."[15] Hejinian's work returns us to that present. In so doing, it shifts things somehow, unleashing once again happiness from the happenstance.

Yet the "pleasurable play" Hejinian brings to her work does not erase suffering. Instead, her work exists alongside it. Take for example *The Unfollowing* (2016), an elegiac book that borrows the sonnet's fourteen lines but disrupts its logic. Hejinian makes each line a non sequitur; as she writes, she "wanted each line to be as difficult to accept on the basis of the previous and subsequent lines as death is for we who are alive."[16] From this strategy emerges a new form of thinking, which, as Tim Wood writes in a review, is "all volta."[17] The mind, which is prone to make connections, is forced here, as throughout Hejinian's work, to leap. In that leaping, we are aware that the meanings we make are provisional and passing, and that's all to the good. Indeed, as Hejinian writes in the preface to *The Unfollowing*, "if logic can't prevail, perhaps hilarity can, as an attribute of a revolutionary practice of everyday life, dismantling control and reforming connectivity."[18]

The Proposition

And yet the pressures on the present are considerable, and the ludic potential in attention feels ever more under threat. Already in 2011, in an essay entitled "Wild Captioning" that addresses the aftermath of the financial crisis and the privatization of public education, Hejinian worries that, faced with such historical reality, "a liberatory, open-ended, nonjudgmental . . . ethos—that of postmodernism in its positive manifestations—is giving way to something less generous or capacious under pressure of a yearning for dependable paradigms, stable fundamentals, and believable authorities."[19]

What might resist this yearning? Hejinian writes hopefully of "late style" (referencing Theodor Adorno and Edward Said), which, she explains, "enters aesthetic practice either late in the biological life of an artist or late in the cultural life of a society, and it is characterized by a release of an unmanageable overflow or surfeit of material into a work that can barely contain it."[20] Such "an overwhelming complexity of experience and thought, along with the emotional excess that accompanies them, is the emanation of the (let us hope dialectical, as well as aporetic) condition of both artistic practice and of political protest today—wherein dedication is not unlinked from pessimism, imagination is not unlinked from reality, love is not unlinked from knowledge."[21]

This late style, and a concomitant renewed commitment to probing the relation between politics and aesthetics, shapes Hejinian's two most recent books. Both *Tribunal* and *Positions of the Sun* address the affective world of allegory and its provisional making of meaning. They are ultimately utopian works, born, through protest, out of a dystopian reality.

Tribunal began in the early days of the Trump campaign. The anxieties of his ascendance permeate the three long sequential poems that compose the book, and as a whole, the book stands in implicit judgment on our "Time of Tyranny." This phrase is the title of the central section, which, like *The Unfollowing*, is composed of sonnet-length poems. Here, though, all the lines are enjambed, as if to emphasize following itself. These poems achieve a continuity of maximal torque, felt especially at moments that indicate belonging or relation at a logically impossible juncture; conjunctions, prepositions, and similes serve not to naturalize connections but to make aporia felt in a text where "Bridges abound or the bridges are out."[22]

"Every situation can be taken as subject to a proposition / at stake at this stage of the state,"[23] but the form of allegorical reading Hejinian's works require is one that "brings about a synchronization, which is by nature short-lived, unstable, and improvisatory."[24] From this synchronicity emerges a "Pathos unfettered / and anarchic,"[25] which Hejinian is adamant to clarify "as indicative of its strength, not its weakness."[26] And allegory, usually seen as an interpretive gesture, "resists interpretation. It is an act, not an exegesis."[27]

Tribunal's poems reveal the connection between *revelry* and *rebellion*. Both derive from the Latin *rebellāre*, and it's through the Old French *reveler*, "to rise up in rebellion," that the verb *revel* comes. I find these poems especially timely now as we emerge from isolation, faced with the work of assessing and collectively reanimating the present.

"We live in toppled times under a feat of tyranny," as Hejinian writes—so how to resist?[28] And how to resist melancholy, which we might think of as the privatization of emotion? As Hejinian writes in *Tribunal*'s final section, "Ring Burial," "Rubble is the quintessential allegorical material, the stuff of figure meanings. / Out of laughter, astonishment spreads, bewilders, demolishes."[29]

Astonishment is the single word I most associate with Hejinian—those who know *My Life* will remember its recurring phrase, "we who 'love to be astonished'"—and the continual surprise of her work thrills me. In *Tribunal*, she urges, "let's not / fake getting lost, let's do it, let's not do it intermittently, let's be / lost, disoriented and never to be bound so all can hear / the hiss of the adverbs we shoot into tyrants' eyes."[30] This is of course a call to enter the collective space of both the book and the street with abandon, and to occupy it together.

It's hard not to feel we "are undertaking / a task too late in the past of the future"; still, she insists, "To revolt is to inquire, to continue as undead."³¹ What matters is *how we live*, and it's in the particularity of our actions—figured above as "adverbs"—that our resistance comes to be felt.

The final poem of the sequence "Time of Tyranny" imagines a world reformed through collective action.

> Together we all devalued the tyranny of value
> of which the Monashee Mountains are but peaks perched on a
>   single branch
> of a boundary marking pine tree, a stack of inches, a time
> frame within which the anxieties of the young are like pigeons
>   ashamed
> before a goose beset by wizening luck and love. Weird
> as cabbage is reminiscence, interpretation donkeys,
>   intersections
> revolve, we play cards and glitter with skepticism which we
>   find
> better than a scythe, it *is* the present directed at our patience.
>   Elusive clouds
> drip, milk generates its own reward of which the plumage
> of any egret is a mere suggestion and muslin a mockery
> which tyranny cannot thaw, torture cannot make
> unkind. On a white bird drawn by chance words are what
> but a trundling shock, come too near, then setting off
> in attendant sparks that ignite a conflagration of opinion.³²

As Hejinian writes, "allegory . . . bears affinities with fantasy. It is immoderately associative, and thus slightly mad. And, unlike the symbolic, it offers little comfort. It is in this respect, as a polemical figure, that it has political potential. Allegory . . . makes things current."³³ And, I think, it *is* a current that moves horizontally through writer and readers alike, through the everyday, charging the moment.

The point of resistance, whether political or aesthetic, isn't just to effect a different future, but also—and perhaps more importantly—to alter the present. "Even if we don't win, right now matters," Hejinian explains in a recent interview. "It really counts what you're doing. Don't postpone the doing of it . . . Part of the mandate of being alive is to actually live your life."³⁴ There is no other place, no other time. It's for this reason that Hejinian ends *Positions of the Sun* with these lines from Wordsworth, thinking back to an earlier moment of revolution:

> Not in Utopia——[...]
> But in the very world which is the world
> Of all of us, the place in which, in the end,
> We find our happiness, or not at all.³⁵

Acknowledgment

This essay was first published by *Public Books*, September 28, 2021. Many thanks to the press for granting permission to reproduce the essay.

Notes

1. Lyn Hejinian, *Tribunal* (Omnidawn, 2019), 69.
2. Lyn Hejinian, *My Life and My Life in the Nineties* (Wesleyan University Press, 2013), 6.
3. From Hejinian's "Pedagogical Notebook," which she shared with my students and me when she visited campus several years ago.
4. Lyn Hejinian, *The Language of Inquiry* (University of California Press, 2000), 203.
5. Hejinian, *Tribunal*, 66.
6. This is the title of a talk Hejinian delivered in 1983; the corresponding essay is published in *The Language of Inquiry*.
7. The word *allegory* doesn't appear even once in *The Language of Inquiry*; at that point, Hejinian emphasized that her work functioned metonymically. See in particular the essay "Strangeness," first published in 1989, for an account of the value she puts on metonymy, which she connects with the paratactical compositional strategies that continue to shape her work. The shift toward allegory first emerges, as far as I can tell, in her 2009 Gailey Lecture at University of California Berkeley, "Positions of the Sun: Latitudes and Lucy Church

The Proposition

Amiably," then in her 2010 essay "Amor Fati" (published in *The Grand Piano, Part X*), and then in her 2011 essay "Wild Captioning," *Qui Parle: Critical Humanities and Social Sciences*, vol. 20, no. 1 (fall/winter 2011). See in particular the latter for an early version of the concerns that culminate in *Positions of the Sun*, in which she considered titling the book "Wild Captioning." After this essay first appeared in *Public Books* in September 2021, Hejinian wrote to me to say that her then forthcoming book from Wesleyan University Press (2023) was to be titled *Allegorical Moments*.
8. Hejinian, *The Language of Inquiry*, 43.
9. Hejinian, *Positions of the Sun*, 162,
10. Hejinian, *Positions of the Sun*, 130.
11. Hejinian, *Positions of the Sun*, 8.
12. Hejinian, *Positions of the Sun*, 65.
13. Hejinian, *Positions of the Sun*, 21.
14. Hejinian, "Wild Captioning," 290.
15. Hejinian, *Positions of the Sun*, 88.
16. Lyn Hejinian, *The Unfollowing* (Omnidawn, 2016), 9.
17. Tim Wood, "All Volta: A Review of Lyn Hejinian's The Unfollowing," *Jacket* 2, November 7, 2016.
18. Hejinian, *The Unfollowing*, 10.
19. Hejinian, "Wild Captioning," 280–1.
20. Hejinian, "Wild Captioning," 280.
21. Hejinian, "Wild Captioning," 283–4.
22. Hejinian, *Positions of the Sun*, 109.
23. Hejinian, *Tribunal*, 35.
24. Hejinian, "Wild Captioning," 291.
25. Hejinian, *Tribunal*, 48.
26. Hejinian, "Wild Captioning," 296.
27. Hejinian, "Wild Captioning," 296.
28. Hejinian, *Tribunal*, 57.
29. Hejinian, *Tribunal*, 64.
30. Hejinian, *Tribunal*, 57.
31. Hejinian, *Tribunal*, 42, 78.
32. Hejinian, *Tribunal*, 58.
33. Hejinian, "Wild Captioning," 286.
34. "'A Fable for Now': Kate Fagan Interviews Lyn Hejinian," *Cordite Poetry Review*, November 1, 2017.
35. Hejinian, *Positions of the Sun*, 159.

Chronology of Works

1966

Journal/Magazine Publication

The Laurel Review, vol. VI, nos. 1 and 2

1967

Journal/Magazine Publication

Poetry Northwest, vol. VII, no. 3
Arts in Society, vol. IV, no. 3
The Eventorium Muse, no. 5
Approach, no. 62
Beloit Poetry Journal, vol. 17, no. 2

1968

Journal/Magazine Publication

Epoch, vol. XVIII, no. 1
The Minnesota Review, vol. VIII, no. 4
The Galley Sail Review, no. 20
Wordjock, no. 4
Cardinal Poetry Quarterly, vol. III, no. 7
The Goodly Co, no. 13
Beloit Poetry Journal, vol. 19, no. 1

1969

Journal/Magazine Publication

Bowery Press Broadsheet 4
Arx, vol. III, no. 5
Quixote, vol. IV, nos. 8 and 9

1970

Work in Anthologies/Collections

Ray Freed, ed., *Doctor Generosity's Almanac: 17 Poets* (New York: Doctor Generosity Press)

Journal/Magazine Publication

Amphora, no. 1
Boss

1971

Journal/Magazine Publication

Beyond Baroque, vol. I, no. 4

1973

Journal/Magazine Publication

Telephone 9

1974

Journal/Magazine Publication

Ironwood 4
Truck 14

1975

Journal/Magazine Publication

Sailing the Road Clear
Telephone 14
Big Deal 4
Newsletter à la Cafard
Occurrence 4
Center 7
Telephone 10

1976

Chapbooks

A Thought is the Bride of What Thinking (Tuumba Press)

Journal/Magazine Publication

Telephone 12

1977

Chapbooks

A Mask of Motion (Burning Deck)

Work in Anthologies/Collections

Stephen Vincent, ed., Omens from the Flight of Birds (San Francisco, CA: Momo's Press)

Journal/Magazine Publication

This 8

1978

Books

Writing is an Aid to Memory (The Figures; reprinted by Sun & Moon, 1996)

Chapbooks

Gesualdo (Tuumba Press)

Work in Anthologies/Collections

Michael Slater, ed., *The Big House* (New York: Ailanthus Press)
Mary Mackay and Mary MacArthur, eds., *These Women!* (Washington, DC: Gallimaufry)

Journal/Magazine Publication

Hills; *Roof*; *Sailing the Road Clear*; *Tottel's* 17

1979

Work in Anthologies/Collections

Carol A. Simone, ed., *Networks* (Palo Alto: Vortex Editions)

Journal/Magazine Publication

Sun & Moon
L=A=N=G=U=A=G=E
Roof
Alembic (UK)
This 9

Critical Prose in Literary Magazines/Journals

L=A=N=G=U=A=G=E

1980

Books

My Life (Burning Deck; first)

Journal/Magazine Publication

QU; This 10

1981

Journal/Magazine Publication

Hills; Sun & Moon; Change (Paris; in French); Action Poetique (Paris; in French); Sulfur

Poetry in Anthologies Published in Other Languages

Fernanda Pivano, ed., Rosa Disibilita (Milan)

1982

Work in Anthologies/Collections

Keith and Rosmarie Waldrop, eds., A Century in Two Decades (Providence: Burning Deck)
Bill Henderson, ed., Pushcart Prize Anthology VI

Journal/Magazine Publication

Annex
Sulfur
Grosseteste Review (UK)

Critical Prose in Literary Magazines/Journals

Poetics Journal 1

1983

Journal/Magazine Publication

This 12

1984

Chapbooks

The Guard (Tuumba Press); *Redo* (Salt-Works Press)

Critical Prose in Anthologies/Collections of Critical Writings

Bob Perelman, ed., *Writing/Talks* (Carbondale: Southern Illinois University Press)

Critical Prose in Literary Magazines/Journals

Poetics Journal 4

Translations Published in Journals/Magazines

Poetics Journal 4 (from French)

1985

Journal/Magazine Publication

Feminist Studies; *Predlog* (Leningrad; in Russian)

Critical Prose in Literary Magazines/Journals

Line 6 (Simon Fraser University, Vancouver, BC, Canada)

Translations Published in Journals/Magazines

Sulfur 14 (from Russian)

1986

Work in Anthologies/Collections

Ron Silliman, ed., *In the American Tree* (Maine: National Poetry Foundation)

Journal/Magazine Publication

Sulfur;
Notes 1 (France)
Parnassus
Poetry in Review
Boundary 2
Ghandabba 4
Bomb;
Temblor 4
Writing (Canada)

Critical Prose in Literary Magazines/Journals

Temblor 3

Translations Published in Journals/Magazines

Bomb (from Russian)

1987

Books

My Life (Sun & Moon Press; expanded version)

Work in Anthologies/Collections

Douglas Messerli, ed., *"Language" Poetries* (New York: New Directions)
Chris and George Tysh, eds., *Everyday Life* (Detroit: In Camera)
George Myers Jr., ed., *Epiphanies: The Prose Poem Now* (Ohio: Cumberland Press)
Andrei Codrescu, ed., *Up Late: American Poetry Since 1970* (New York: Four Walls Eight Windows)

Journal/Magazine Publication

Ghandabba 5
Caliban 2
Ironwood 30
Gendaishi Techo (Tokyo; in Japanese)
Sink 3
Occident, vol. CII, no. 1

Translations Published in Journals/Magazines

Sulfur 19 (from Russian)
Ironwood 30 (from Russian)

1988

Volumes of Collaboratively Composed Poetry/Prose

Individuals (written with Kit Robinson; Chax Press)

Work in Anthologies/Collections

Leslie Scalapino, O One (Oakland: O Books)
Bill Henderson, ed., Pushcart Prize Anthology XII

Poetry in Anthologies Published in Other Languages

Marat Akchurin, ed., Double Rainbow/Dvoinaya Raduga (Moscow: Molodaya Gvardiya)

Journal/Magazine Publication

Tyuonyi 4; Dagens Nyheter (in Swedish)

Critical Prose in Anthologies/Collections of Critical Writings

Robert Frank and Henry Sayre, eds., The Line in Postmodern Poetry (Urbana and Chicago: University of Illinois Press)

Critical Prose in Literary Magazines/Journals

Social Text 19/20 (with Barrett Watten, Carla Harryman, Bob Perelman, Steve Benson, Ron Silliman)
Jimmy's and Lucy's House of K 6

Translations Published in Journals/Magazines

Zyzzyva (from Russian)
Everyday Life 2 (from Russian)
Avec 1 (from Russian)
New American Writing 4 (from Russian)

1989

Journal/Magazine Publication

Paper Air, vol. 4, no. 2; *zuk* 17 (France; in French); *Rodnik* (Riga, Latvia; in Russian); *Mirage* 3; *o-blek* 5, spring 1989; *Sonora Review*; *Motel* 1 (Canada); *screens and tasted parallels* 1; *Artes* 4 (Stockholm; in Swedish); *Action Poetique* 117 (France; in French); *New American Writing* 5

Critical Prose in Literary Magazines/Journals

Paper Air, vol. 4, no. 2
Poetics Journal 8
Revista Canaria de Estudos Ingleses 18

Critical Prose in Literary Magazines/Journals

Stilistika i Poetika (in Russian; Moscow State Institute of Foreign Languages)
Delo, vol. 35, no. 8 (Belgrade, Yugoslavia)

Translations Published in Journals/Magazines

Paper Air, vol. 4, no. 2 (from Russian)
Michigan Quarterly Review, vol. xxviii, no. 4 (from Russian)

1990

Journal/Magazine Publication

Big Allis 2; Aerial 5; Archive Newsletter, no. 45; Sequoia, vol. 33, no. 2; Verse, vol. 7, no. 1 UK); Raddle Moon 9 (Canada); Five Fingers Review 8/9; Polja (Belgrade, Yugoslavia; in Serbian)

Introductions/Afterwords

"Introduction" to Martha Casanave, Past Lives (Boston, MA: David Godine)

Critical Prose in Literary Magazines/Journals

Artes 2 (in Swedish)

Volumes of Translation

Description, poems by Arkadii Dragomoshchenko (Los Angeles, CA: Sun & Moon Press)

Translations Published in Journals/Magazines

Bastard Review 3/4 (from Russian)
Five Fingers Review 8/9 (from Russian)

1991

Books

Oxota: A Short Russian Novel (The Figures; revised version published by Wesleyan University Press, 2019)

Chapbooks

The Hunt (Zasterle Press [Canary Islands, Spain]; section of Oxota: A Short Russian Novel)

Poetry in Anthologies Published in Other Languages

Emmanuel Hocquard and Claude Royet-Journoud, eds., 49 + 1 (Paris: Editions Royaumont)

Journal/Magazine Publication

Pequod 31; *Avec* 4; *Hot Bird Mfg.*, vol. 1, no. 17; *Meanjin*, vol. 50, no. 1 (Melbourne, Australia); *Socialist Review*, vol. 21, no. 9; *Logos* (Leningrad), vol. 1; *East Bay Guardian*; *Aerial* 6/7; *o·blek* 9

Volumes of Critical Writing

Leningrad, written with Michael Davidson, Ron Silliman, Barrett Watten (San Francisco, CA: Mercury House)

Critical Prose in Literary Magazines/Journals

Poetics Journal 9
Gradina 2–3 (in Serbian; Nish, Yugoslavia)

Translations Published in Journals/Magazines

Pequod 31 (from Russian)
screens and tasted parallels 2 (from Russian)

1992

Books

The Cell (Sun & Moon Press)

Volumes of Poetry Translated and Published in Other Languages

Jour de Chasse (*The Hunt*), translated into French by Pierre Alferi (Paris: Cahiers de Royaumont)

Work in Anthologies/Collections

Anne Waldman, ed., *Out of This World* (New York: Crown Publishers)
Lou Robinson and Camille Norton, eds., *Resurgent: New Writing by Women* (Urbana & Chicago: Illinois University Press)

Poetry in Anthologies Published in Other Languages

Esteban Pujals Gesali, ed., *La Lengua Radical* (Madrid: Gramma Poesia)

Dubravka Đjurić, ed., *Ruski Almanac* (Belgrade)

Journal/Magazine Publication

Black Warrior Review, 18, 2
Obdje (in Serbian)
The World 45

Anthologized Translations

Kent Johnson and Stephen M. Ashby, eds., *Third Wave: The New Russian Poetry* (Ann Arbor: University of Michigan Press)

Translations Published in Journals/Magazines

Grand Street 40 (from Russian)

1993

Journal/Magazine Publication

Green Z 12; *Grand Street* 44; *lingo*; *Prosodia* 3; *Black Bread* 3; *Hot Bird Mfg.*, vol. II, no. 2

Work in Anthologies/Collections

Leslie Scalapino, ed., *Subliminal Time* (Berkeley, CA: O Books)

Translations Published in Journals/Magazines

lingo (from Russian)

1994

Books

The Cold of Poetry (Sun & Moon Press)

Work in Anthologies/Collections

Artes: An International Reader of Literature, Art, and Music (New Jersey: Ecco Press and Stockholm: Natur & Kultur)

Paul Hoover, ed., *Postmodern American Poetries, A Norton Anthology* (New York: W. W. Norton & Co.)

Douglas Messerlied, *From the Other Side of the Century: A New American Poetry 1960–1990* (Sun & Moon Press)

A. R. Ammons, ed., *The Best American Poetry: 1994* (New York: Simon and Schuster)

Journal/Magazine Publication

Sojourner, vol. 19, no. 6
Black Bread 4 (collaboration with Leslie Scalapino)
Prosodia
Tessera, vol. 15 (collaboration with Carla Harryman)
River City, vol. 14, no. 2
lingo 3
Proliferation 1
Raddle Moon 13
Southern Review, vol. 27, no. 3
Chelsea 57

Critical Prose in Anthologies/Collections of Critical Writings

Manuel Brito, ed., *A Suite of Poetic Voices* (Santa Brigida: Kadle Books)

Critical Prose in Literary Magazines/Journals

Sojourner, vol. 19, no. 6
Southern Review, vol. 27, no. 3 (Australia)

Volumes of Translation

Xenia, poems by Arkadii Dragomoshchenko (Sun & Moon Press)

1995

Work in Anthologies/Collections

Douglas Messerli, ed., *50" A Celebration of Sun & Moon Classics* (Los Angeles, CA: Sun & Moon Press)
Douglas Messerli, ed., *The Gertrude Stein Awards in Innovative American Poetry, 1993–1994* (Los Angeles, CA: Sun & Moon Press)
John Kinsella, ed., *A Salt Reader* (Perth, Western Australia: Salt)

Journal/Magazine Publication

Zurgai (in English and Spanish, translated by Manuel Brito)
Berkeley Poetry Review
Proliferation 2
Chain 2
tinfish
Volt 2
Antenym
Antithesis, vol. 7, no. 2

Volumes of Critical Writing

Two Stein Talks (Santa Fe, NM: Weaselsleeves Press)

Critical Prose in Anthologies/Collections of Critical Writings

Anne Waldman and Andrew Schelling, eds., *Disembodied Poetics*, (Albuquerque: University of New Mexico Press)

Critical Prose in Literary Magazines/Journals

Freemantle Arts Review, vol. 10, no. 1 (Perth, Western Australia)

Anthologized Translations

Ellen E. Berry and Anesa Miller-Pogacar, *Re-Entering the Sign: Articulating New Russian Culture* (Ann Arbor: University of Michigan Press)

Work in Other Media: Visual Art

"The Eye of Enduring" (collaboration with Diane Andrews Hall, exhibited at Sherrill Haines Gallery [San Francisco])

1996

Books

Guide, Grammar, Watch, and The Thirty Nights (Folio [Salt]; Perth, Western Australia)

Chapbooks

The Little Book of A Thousand Eyes (Smoke-Proof Press)

Volumes of Collaboratively Composed Poetry/Prose

Wicker (written with Jack Collom: Rodent Press)

Work in Anthologies/Collections

Maggie O'Sullivan, ed., *Out of Everywhere* (London: Reality Street Editions)

Journal/Magazine Publication

Phoebe, vol. 25
Chain 3
lyric &
New American Writing 14
Chicago Review, vol. 42, no. 2
Iowa Review, vol. 26, no. 2
trembling ladders, issues 2 and 3 (Australia)
The World 52

Critical Prose in Anthologies/Collections of Critical Writings

Larry McCaffery and Brian McHale, eds., *Some Other Frequency: Interviews with Innovative American Authors* (Philadelphia: University of Pennsylvania Press)

Peter Baker, ed., *Onward: Contemporary Poetry & Poetics* (New York: Peter Lang)

Critical Prose in Literary Magazines/Journals

Private Arts 10

1997

Journal/Magazine Publication

Private Arts 10
Hambone 13
Terra Nova, vol. 2, no. 2
Prosodia 7
Explosive Magazine 2
Modern Language Studies 27.2
Bellingham Review, vol. xx, no. 1
The Germ

Work in Other Media: Music

John Zorn, *New Traditions in Far East Asian Bar Band Music* (text for "Que Tran"; Electra/Nonesuch)

1998

Volumes of Collaboratively Composed Poetry/Prose

The Traveler and the Hill and the Hill (in collaboration with Emilie Clark; Granary Books)

Work in Anthologies/Collections

Jerome Rothenberg and Pierre Joris, eds., *Poems for the Millennium* (Berkeley: University of California Press)
Mary Margaret Sloan, ed., *Moving Borders: Three Decades of Innovative Writing by Women* (Talisman Press)

Poetry in Anthologies Published in Other Languages

José Roberto O'Shea, ed., *Poesía Pía de Poesía Norte-Americana Contemporânea* (Florianópolis, Brazil: Editora da UFSC)

Pascal Boulanger, ed., *Une "Action Poétique"* (Paris: Flammarion)

Journal/Magazine Publication

Lingo 8

Critical Prose in Anthologies/Collections of Critical Writings

Christopher Beach, ed. (Tuscaloosa: University of Alabama Press)

Critical Prose in Literary Magazines/Journals

Shark 1
Poetics Journal 10

Work in Other Media: Film

"Letters Not About Love" (feature film directed by Jacki Ochs with script based on correspondence between Lyn Hejinian and Arkadii Dragomoshchenko; premier, South by Southwest Film Festival, First Prize: Documentary)

1999

Volumes of Collaboratively Composed Poetry/Prose

Sight (written with Leslie Scalapino; Edge Books)

Journal/Magazine Publication

Shiny 9/10
Boundary 2
The Colorado Review, fall/winter

The Proposition

Critical Prose in Anthologies/Collections of Critical Writings

Sture Allén, ed., *Translation of Poetry and Poetic Prose* (Stockholm: Swedish Academy and World Scientific)

2000

Books

The Beginner (Spectacular Books)
Happily (Post-Apollo Press)

Volumes of Collaboratively Composed Poetry/Prose

Chartings (written with Ray Di Palma; Chax Press)
Sunflower (written with Jack Collom; The Figures)

Volumes of Critical Writing

The Language of Inquiry (Berkeley: University of California Press)

Critical Prose in Anthologies/Collections of Critical Writings

Ron Padgett, ed., *World Poets* (New York: Scribners, The Scribner Writers Series)
Molly McQuade, ed., *By Herself: Women Reclaim Poetry* (Saint Paul, MN: Graywolf Press)

Anthologized Translations

John High, ed., *Crossing Centuries: The New Generation in Russian Poetry* (Jersey City: Talisman House Publishers)

Work in Other Media: Visual Art

"The Traveler and the Hill and the Hill" (two-person exhibition, Museo Nazionale dell'Architettura, Ferrara [Italy])

2001

Books

A Border Comedy (Granary Books)

Volumes of Poetry Translated and Published in Other Languages

Mit Liv (*My Life*), translated into Danish by Jeppe Brixvold with Line Brandt (Copenhagen: Borgen)

Work in Anthologies/Collections

Robert Hass, ed., *The Best American Poetry: 2000* (NY: Scribner's)

Poetry in Anthologies Published in Other Languages

Vladimir Kopicl and Dubravka Đjurić, eds., *Antologija novije američke poezije* (Belgrade)

Work in Other Media: Visual Art

"Poetry Plastique" (mixed media drawings, in group exhibition, Marianne Boesky Gallery [New York])

2002

Books

Slowly (Tuumba Press)
The Beginner (Tuumba Press; republication of Spectacular Books edition, 2000)

Work in Anthologies/Collections

Ruth Lepson and Lynne Yamaguchi, eds., *Poetry from Sojourner: A Feminist Anthology* (Urbana and Chicago: University of Illinois Press)

Journal/Magazine Publication

580 Split

Crowd
Meanjin, vol. 61, no. 3 (Australia)
Antennae 3
Rapidfeed
Barrow Street
Journal for Theoretical Studies in Media and Culture
Discourse 24.1: "Mortals to Death"

Critical Prose in Literary Magazines/Journals

Kiosk 1

2003

Books

My Life in the Nineties (Shark Books; reprinted in *My Life and My Life in the Nineties* [2013])
The Fatalist (Omnidawn Books)

Volumes of Collaboratively Composed Poetry/Prose

On Laughter: A Melodrama (with Jack Collom; Baksun Books)

Work in Anthologies/Collections

Jahan Ramazani, Richard Ellman, and Robert O'Clair, eds., *Norton Anthology of Modern and Contemporary Poetry* (vol. 2: *Contemporary*; New York: Norton)
David Lehman, ed., *Great American Prose Poems: From Poe to the Present* (New York: Scribner's)
Dana Gioia, Chryss Yost, and Jack Hicks, eds., *California Poetry: From the Gold Rush to the Present* (Berkeley, CA: Heyday Books)

Journal/Magazine Publication

Van Gogh's Ear (Paris, France)
Sal Mimeo
Bomb
Conjunctions: 40

Introductions/Afterwords

"Afterword" to Viktor Shklovsky, *Third Factory* (Dalkey Archive Press)

Critical Prose in Literary Magazines/Journals

Salt: An International Journal of Poetry and Poetics, vol. 14

Work in Other Media: Music

Poetry and Playing (text for CD by British avant-garde guitarist Derek Bailey)

2004

Volumes of Collaboratively Composed Poetry/Prose

The Lake (with Emilie Clark; Granary Books)

Volumes of Poetry Translated and Published in Other Languages

Mitt Liv (*My Life* and *My Life in the Nineties*), translated into Swedish by Niclas Nilsson (Stockholm: Modernista)

Work in Anthologies/Collections

Robert Hass and Jessica Fisher, eds., *The Addison Street Project* (Heyday Books)

Journal/Magazine Publication

Hambone 17
Fire no. 23 (Oxford, England)
Pom2
ZYZZYVA
Action Restreinte (translated into French by Martin Richet)
PEN America: A Journal for Writers and Readers, issue 5: Silences
Conjunctions: Cinema Lingua
Rattapallax

Introductions/Afterwords

"Introduction" to Gertrude Stein, *Three Lives* (Los Angeles, CA: Green Integer)

Work in Other Media: Visual Art

"Poetry and its Arts: Bay Area Interactions 1954–2004" (mixed media drawings in group exhibition at the California Historical Society [San Francisco], curated by The Poetry Center [SF State University])

2005

Chapbooks

Lola (Belladonna)

Work in Anthologies/Collections

Rod Mengham and John Kinsella, eds., *Vanishing Points: New Modernist Poems* (Cambridge, England: Salt Publishing)

Journal/Magazine Publication

Court Green 2
Berkeley Poetry Review
Fulcrum: An Annual of Poetry and Aesthetics

2006

Volumes of Poetry Translated and Published in Other Languages

Lentement (*Slowly*), translated into French by Virginie Poitrasson (Paris, France: Format Américain/Un bureau sur l'Atlantique)

Work in Anthologies/Collections

Denise Duhamel, Maureen Seaton, and David Trinidad, eds., *Saints of Hysteria: A Half-Century of Collaborative American Poetry* (Brooklyn, NY: Soft Skull Press)

Lytle Shaw, ed., *Nineteen Lines: A Drawing Center Writing Anthology* (New York: Roof Books)
David Lehman, ed., *The Oxford Book of American Poetry* (Oxford University Press)
Stephanie Young, ed., *Bay Poetics* (Faux Press)
Lynn McMahon and Averill Curdy, eds., *The Longman Anthology of Poetry* (Pearson/Longman)
Paul Muldoon, ed., *Best American Poetry 2005* (New York: Scribner's)

Poetry in Anthologies Published in Other Languages

Luigi Ballerini and Paul Vangelisti, eds., *Nuova Poesia Americana* (Milan: Mondadori)

Journal/Magazine Publication

Traffic
Nea Synteleia (Athens, Greece)
Conjunctions: 25th Anniversary
Coconut (online journal)
The Grand Piano, Part One (co-authored with Rae Armantrout, Steve Benson, Carla Harryman, Tom Mandel, Ted Pearson, Bob Perelman, Kit Robinson, Ron Silliman, and Barrett Watten; Detroit: Mode A)

Critical Prose in Anthologies/Collections of Critical Writings

Joan Retallack and Juliana Spahr, eds., *Poetry and Pedagogy* (Palgrave Macmillan)
Jerry Harp and Jan Weismiller, eds., *A Poetry Criticism Reader* (Iowa City: University of Iowa Press)
Deborah Brown, Annie Finch, and Maxine Kumin, eds., *Lofty Dogmas: Poets on Poetics* (University of Arkansas Press)

Critical Prose in Literary Magazines/Journals

Cabinet 20

Exhibition Catalogue Texts

Heike Liss, *Away at Home* (New York: CUE Art Foundation)

2007

Journal/Magazine Publication

Cal Literary Arts Magazine
Zoland Poetry: An Annual of Poems, Translations & Interviews
The Grand Piano, Part Two, Part Three, Part Four, and *Part Five* (co-authored with Rae Armantrout, Steve Benson, Carla Harryman, Tom Mandel, Ted Pearson, Bob Perelman, Kit Robinson, Ron Silliman, and Barrett Watten; Detroit: Mode A)

Critical Prose in Anthologies/Collections of Critical Writings

Tony Lopez and Anthony Caleshu, eds, *Poetry and Public Language* (Exeter, UK: Shearsman Books)

Critical Prose in Literary Magazines/Journals

Zoland Poetry: An Annual of Poems, Translations & Interviews
Cal Literary Arts Magazine

2008

Books

Saga/Circus (Omnidawn Publishing)

Volumes of Collaboratively Composed Poetry/Prose

Situations, Sings (written with Jack Collom; Adventures in Poetry)

Work in Anthologies/Collections

Jeff Hilson, ed., *The Reality Street Book of Sonnets* (Hastings, UK: Reality Street Editions)

Journal/Magazine Publication

Colorado Review 35.3
No: a journal of the arts 7
Abraham Lincoln 3
Bombay Gin, vol. 34
Parmentier, vol. 17, no. 2, spring (translated into Dutch by Ton van't Hof)
Conjunctions 50: *Fifty Contemporary Writers*, spring
The Grand Piano, Part Six and *Part Seven* (co-authored with Rae Armantrout, Steve Benson, Carla Harryman, Tom Mandel, Ted Pearson, Bob Perelman, Kit Robinson, Ron Silliman, and Barrett Watten; Detroit: Mode A)

2009

Volumes of Poetry Translated and Published in Other Languages

Gesualdo, translated into French by Martin Richet (Marseilles: Jacataqua)

Work in Anthologies/Collections

Cole Swensen and David St. John, eds., *American Hybrid: A Norton Anthology of New Poetry* (New York: W. W. Norton & Co.)
Eva Salzman and Amy Wack, eds., *Women's Work: Modern Women Poets Writing in English* (Bridgend, Wales: Seren)

Journal/Magazine Publication

Nathaniel Mackey, ed., *Hambone* 19
MIR: Revue d'Anticipation (in French, translated by Martin Richet)
Parthenon West Review 6
Kulturo no. 29: Tema: Sociale Fantasier (Copenhagen, Denmark)
Belladonna Elders Series, no. 5

Critical Prose in Anthologies/Collections of Critical Writings

The Grand Piano, Part Eight (co-authored with Rae Armantrout, Steve Benson, Carla Harryman, Tom Mandel, Ted Pearson, Bob

Perelman, Kit Robinson, Ron Silliman, Barrett Watten, and Alan Bernheimer; Detroit: Mode A)

The Grand Piano, Part Nine (co-authored with Rae Armantrout, Steve Benson, Carla Harryman, Tom Mandel, Ted Pearson, Bob Perelman, Kit Robinson, Ron Silliman, and Barrett Watten; Detroit: Mode A)

Steve Shoemaker, ed., *Thinking Poetics: Essays on George Oppen (Modern and Contemporary Poetics)* (Tuscaloosa: University of Alabama)

Rebecca Woolf et al., eds., *A Best of Fence: The First Nine Years* (Fence Books)

Critical Prose in Literary Magazines/Journals

Rooms Outlast Us 1 (essay collaboratively written with 11 University of California-Berkeley graduate students)

Novoe literaturnoe obozrenie, no. 113 (in Russian, Arkadii Dragomoshchenko, trans.)

Pro Femina 46–50 (in Serbian; Belgrade)

Critical Essays Published in Academic Journals

English Language Notes 47.1 (special issue on "Experimental Literary Education")

2010

Volumes of Collaboratively Composed Poetry/Prose

The Wide Road (written with Carla Harryman; Belladonna)

Journal/Magazine Publication

Bradford Morrow, ed., *Conjunctions: Urban Arias*

Critical Prose in Anthologies/Collections of Critical Writings

The Grand Piano, Part Ten (co-authored with Rae Armantrout, Steve Benson, Carla Harryman, Tom Mandel, Ted Pearson, Bob Perelman, Kit Robinson, Ron Silliman, and Barrett Watten; Detroit: Mode A)

2011

Chapbooks

Selections from The Unfollowed (Kavyayantra Press)

Volumes of Poetry Translated and Published in Other Languages

Mi Vida (*My Life*), translated into Spanish by Pilar Vazquez and Esteban Pujals (Tenerife, Spain: Acto Ediciones)

Poetry in Anthologies Published in Other Languages

Manuel Brito, ed. and translated by, *Los Mejores Poetas Americanos Contemporános: Charles Bernstein, Lyn Hejinian, Ron Silliman, Barrett Watten* (Madrid: Ediciones Literarias Mandala)

Journal/Magazine Publication

Bombay Gin, vol. 37, no. 2
Volt 16
Grist: The Journal for Writers, no. 4

Critical Essays Published in Academic Journals

Qui Parle, vol. 20, no. 1

2012

Books

The Book of a Thousand Eyes (Omnidawn Books)

Volumes of Poetry Translated and Published in Other Languages

Mi Vida (*My Life*), translated into Spanish by Tatiana Lipkes (Mexico City, Mexico: Mangos de Hacha)
from My Life, translated into Japanese by Junichi Koizumi, Toshiro (Shige) Inoue, Mamoru Mukaiyama, and Koichiro Yamauchi (Tokyo: Meltemia Press)

Work in Anthologies/Collections

Joshua Corey and G. C. Waldrep, eds., *The Arcadia Project: Postmodern Pastoral* (Boise, ID: Ahsahta Press)

Journal/Magazine Publication

American Poet, vol. 42
Conjunctions 58: Riveted: The Obsession Issue
Vincent Broqua and Jean-Jacques Poucel, eds., *FPC* (*Formes Poétiques Contemporaines*; Presses Universitaires du Nouveau Monde)
Armed Cell 3
FLOOR: A Journal of Aesthetic Experiment

2013

Books

My Life and My Life in the Nineties (Wesleyan University Press)

Volumes of Poetry Translated and Published in Other Languages

Felizmente (*Happily*), translated into Spanish by Gidi Loza (Playas de Rosarito, Baja, CA: Editorial Piedra Cuervo)

Work in Anthologies/Collections

Paul Hoover, ed., *Postmodern American Poetry: A Norton Anthology* (second edition) (New York: W. W. Norton & Company, Inc.)
Robert Pinsky, ed., *The Best of the Best American Poetry* (New York: Scribner Poetry)

Journal/Magazine Publication

Lisa Schmidley, ed., *Jelly Bucket*

Edited Volumes

(with Barrett Watten) *A Guide to Poetics Journal: Writing in the Expanded Field, 1982–98* (University Presses of New England/ Wesleyan University Press)

Critical Prose in Literary Magazines/Journals

Translit 13: Shkola Yazika (in Russian; translated by E. Suslovoy; Saint Petersburg, Russia)

Critical Prose in Anthologies/Collections of Critical Writings

Paul Hoover, ed., *Postmodern American Poetry: A Norton Anthology* (second edition) (New York: W. W. Norton & Company, Inc.)

2014

Volumes of Poetry Translated and Published in Other Languages

Minha Vida (*My Life*), translated into Portuguese by Mauricio Salles Vasconcelos (Sao Paolo, Brazil: Dobra Editorial)

Work in Anthologies/Collections

Bill Henderson, general editor, *Pushcart Prize XXXIX: Best of the Small Presses* (Wainscott, NY: Pushcart)

Journal/Magazine Publication

Hysteria, issue 1, ed. Bjork Grue Lidin (London)
Jessica L. Wilkinson and Ali Alizaden, eds., *Axon: Creative Explorations*, vol. 4, no. 2 (Australia)
Mantis: A Journal of Poetry, Criticism & Translation 12

2015

Volumes of Poetry Translated and Published in Other Languages

Gesualdo, translated into Turkish by Uygar Asan (Kadikoy, Turkey: Nod)

Work in Anthologies/Collections

Tamar Brazis, ed., *365 Poems for Every Occasion* (New York: Academy of American Poets)

Journal/Magazine Publication

Matvei Yankelevich, ed., *6 x 6* #32 (Ugly Duckling Presse)
Revista La Otra 98 (Mexico City; in Spanish; translated by Joseph Mulligan and Mario Domínguez Parra)
Jongler 1 (Paris, France; in French; translated by Martin Richet)
Jongler 2 (Paris, France; in French; translated by Martin Richet)
Boston Review, March
Vlak 5

Edited Volumes

(with Barrett Watten) *Poetics Journal Digital Archive* (ebook; Wesleyan University Press)

2016

Books

The Unfollowing (Omnidawn Books)

Volumes of Poetry Translated and Published in Other Languages

Ma Vie (*My Life*), translated into French by Maïtreyi and Nicolas Pesquès (Dijon: Presses du réel)

Work in Anthologies/Collections

Manuel Brito, ed., *The Canary Islands Connection: 60 Contemporary Poets* (Las Palmas de Gran Canaria, Spain: Zasterle Press)
Douglas Messerli, ed., in *The Pip Anthology of World Poetry of the 21st Century*, vol. 10; http://greeninteger.com/pdfs/010-poetry-anthology.pdf

Journal/Magazine Publication

Andrew David King et al, eds., *The Berkeley Poetry Review* 43
Larry Fagin, ed., *The Delineator*
Tuli & Savu, no. 86: *LAITOS* (Helsinki, Finland; in Finnish; translated by Anna Tomi)
Jacataqua (Paris, France; in French; translated by Martin Richet)
Poetry International 20 and 21 (double issue)
Daniel Y. Harries, Irene Koronas, and Gloria Mindock, eds., *X-Peri*

Volumes of Critical Writing

Det öppna och det säregna (*The Language of Inquiry*); translated into Swedish by Camilla Hammarström (Stockholm: Bokförlaget Lejd)

Critical Essays Published in Academic Journals

Contemporary Women's Writing, vol. 10, no. 1 (Oxford University Press)

2017

Work in Anthologies/Collections

Danielle Legros Georges, ed., *City of Notions: An Anthology of Contemporary Boston Poems* (Boston, MA: Mayor's Office of Arts and Culture)

Journal/Magazine Publication

Kaplan Harris and Ben Lerner, issue eds., *Critical Quarterly* (vol. 59, no. 2)
The Spectacle, issue 3 (online publication; thespectacle.wustl.edu)

Critical Prose in Anthologies/Collections of Critical Writings

Charles Altieri and Nicholas D. Nace, eds., *The Fate of Difficulty in the Poetry of Our Time* (Evanston, IL: Northwestern University Press)

2018

Volumes of Poetry Translated and Published in Other Languages

Fatalisten (*The Fatalist*), translated into Danish by Alexander Carnera (Copenhagen: Det Poetiske Bureaus Forlag)
Pauza, rosa, chto-to na bumage (*A Pause, a Rose, Something on Paper/My Life*), translated into Russian by Ruslan Miranov (Moscow: *Hosorog*, no. 7)

Journal/Magazine Publication

Hyperallergic (online publication: https://hyperallergic.com/445870/one-poem-by-lyn-hejinian/)

2019

Books

Tribunal (Omnidawn Books)
Oxota: A Short Russian Novel (Wesleyan University Press; revised from first edition [The Figures, 1991])
Positions of the Sun (New York: Belladonna Books)

Volumes of Poetry Translated and Published in Other Languages

Mi Vide en Los Noventa (*My Life in theNineties*), translated into Spanish by Patricio Grinberg and Carla Chinski (Buenos Aires, Argentina: Zindo & Gafuri)

Critical Prose in Anthologies/Collections of Critical Writings

Jeanne Heuving and Tyrone Williams, eds., *Inciting Poetics: Thinking and Writing Poetry* (Albuquerque: University of New Mexico Press)

Exhibition Catalogue Texts

Diane Hall, *In Time* (San Francisco, CA: Rena Bransten Gallery)

2020

Journal/Magazine Publication

Colorado Review 47.3

2021

Volumes of Collaboratively Composed Poetry/Prose

Hearing (written with Leslie Scalapino; Litmus Press)

Contributors

Charles Altieri retired in July 2021 after fifty-three years of delightful university teaching. One of the most satisfying of those years involved team-teaching with Lyn. In addition to teaching he wrote several books, the latest of which are *Literature, Education, Society: Bridging the Gap* (2022) and *Modernist Poetry and the Limitations of Materialist Theory* (2021).

Emily Critchley is the author of fourteen poetry collections, including *Home* (2021), *Arrangements* (2018), and *Ten Thousand Things* (2017). She is also editor of *Out of Everywhere 2: Linguistically Innovative Poetry by Women in North America & the UK* (2016) and co-editor of *#MeToo: A Poetry Collective* (Chicago Review, summer, 2018). Emily is Associate Professor in English and Creative Writing at the University of Greenwich. She lives in London with her daughter.

Jacob Edmond is a professor of English at the University of Otago. He is the author of *Make It the Same: Poetry in the Age of Global Media* (2019) and *A Common Strangeness: Contemporary Poetry, Cross-Cultural Encounter, Comparative Literature* (2012).

Jessica Fisher is the author of *Frail-Craft (2007)* which won the 2006 Yale Younger Poets Prize, and *Inmost* (2012) which was awarded the 2011 Nightboat Poetry Prize. A third book, *Daywork*, will be published in 2024. Her poems, essays, and translations appear in such journals as *The American Poetry Review*, *The Believer*, *The Bennington Review*, *The Colorado Review*, *McSweeney's*, *The New Yorker*, *The New York Review of Books*, *The Paris Review*, *Public Books*, *The Threepenny Review*, *Tin House*, and *TriQuarterly*. Her honors include the Rome Prize in Literature, a

Holloway Postdoctoral Fellowship in Poetry, and a research grant from the Hellman Foundation. She holds a PhD from University of California at Berkeley and is currently an associate professor at Williams College.

Lytle Shaw's books include *Frank O'Hara: The Poetics of Coterie* (2013), *Fieldworks: From Place to Site in Postwar Poetics* (2013), *Narrowcast: Poetry and Audio Research* (2018), and *New Grounds for Dutch Landscape* (2021). He is Professor of English at NYU and a contributing editor for *Cabinet* magazine.

Bibliography

Altieri, Charles. "Lyn Hejinian and the Possibilities of Postmodernism in Poetry." In *Women Poets of the Americas: Toward a Pan-American Gathering*, edited by Jacqueline Vaught Brogan and Cordelia Chavez Candelaria, 146–55. Notre Dame, IN: University of Notre Dame Press, 1999.

Altieri, Charles. "What Is Living and What Is Dead in American Postmodernism: Establishing the Contemporaneity of Some American Poetry." *Critical Inquiry* 22, no. 4 (1996): 764–89.

Boym, Svetlana. "Estrangement as a Lifestyle: Shklovsky and Brodsky." *Poetics Today* 17, no. 4 (1996): 511–30.

Dworkin, Craig. "Penelope Reworking the Twill: Patchwork, Writing, and Lyn Hejinian's *My Life*." *Contemporary Literature* 36, no. 1 (1995): 58–81.

Edmond, Jacob. "Locating Global Resistance: The Landscape Poetics of Arkadii Dragomoshchenko, Lyn Hejinian and Yang Lian." *AUMLA: Journal of the Australasian Universities Language and Literature Association* 101 (2004): 71–98.

Edmond, Jacob. "'A Meaning Alliance': Arkady Dragomoshchenko and Lyn Hejinian's Poetics of Translation." *Slavic and East European Journal* 46, no. 3 (2002): 551–63.

Erlich, Viktor. *Russian Formalism: History-Doctrine*. The Hague: Mouton, 1955.

Fredman, Stephen. "Lyn Hejinian's Inquiry into the Relationship between Language and the Person." *West Coast Line* 36 (2001): 60–72.

Hejinian, Lyn. Afterword to *Third Factory*, by Viktor Shklovsky, 99–106. Translated by Richard Sheldon. Chicago, IL: Dalkey Archive, 2002.

Hejinian, Lyn. *The Cold of Poetry*. Los Angeles, CA: Sun and Moon, 1994.

Hejinian, Lyn. The Guard. 1984. In Hejinian, *Cold of Poetry*, 11–37.
Hejinian, Lyn. *The Language of Inquiry*. Berkeley: University of California Press, 2000.
Hejinian, Lyn. Lyn Hejinian Papers. MSS 74. Mandeville Special Collections Library, University of California, San Diego.
Hejinian, Lyn. *My Life*. 1987 ed. Los Angeles, CA: Green Integer, 2002.
Hejinian, Lyn. "The Person." In Hejinian, *Cold of Poetry*, 143–96.
Hejinian, Lyn. "Po tu storonu konechnosti: Pamiati Arkadiia Dragomoshchenko" [On the other side of finiteness: In memory of Arkadii Dragomoshchenko]. Translated by Aleksandr Skidan. *Novoe literaturnoe obozrenie* 121, no. 3 (2013). https://www.nlobooks.ru/magazines/novoe_literaturnoe_obozrenie/121_nlo_3_2013/article/10445
Hejinian, Lyn. "Roughly Stapled." Interview by Craig Dworkin. *Idiom* 3 (1995). Available from the Electronic Poetry Center. https://writing.upenn.edu/epc/authors/hejinian/roughly.html
Izenberg, Oren. "Language Poetry and Collective Life." *Critical Inquiry* 30 (2003): 132–59.
Jameson, Fredric. *The Prison-House of Language: A Critical Account of Structuralism and Russian Formalism*. Princeton, NJ: Princeton University Press, 1972.
Janecek, Gerald. "Lin Khedzhinian perevodit Arkadiia Dragomoshchenko" [Lyn Hejinian translates Arkadii Dragomoshchenko]. In *Po materialam mezhdunarodnoi konferentsii-festivalia "Poeticheskii iazyk rubezha XX–XXI vekov i sovremennye literaturnye strategii,"* 293–301. Moscow: Institut russkogo iazyka im. V. V. Vinogradova, 2004.
Matejka, Ladislav. "The Formal Method and Linguistics." In *Readings in Russian Poetics: Formalist and Structuralist Views*, edited by Ladislav Matejka and Krystyna Pomorska, 281–95. Ann Arbor: Michigan Slavic Publications, 1978.
Nicholls, Peter. "Phenomenal Poetics: Reading Lyn Hejinian." In *Postwar American Poetry: The Mechanics of the Mirage*, edited by Christine Pagnoulle and Michel Delville, 241–52. Liège: University of Liège, 2000.
Pavlov, Evgeny. "Here and There: Some Reflections on Translating Arkadii Dragomoshchenko." *Sport* 28 (2002): 169–75. https://nzetc.victoria.ac.nz/tm/scholarly/tei-Ba28Spo-t1-body-d24.html

Perelman, Bob. "Polemic Greeting to the Inhabitants of Utopia." In *Assembling Alternatives: Reading Postmodern Poetries Transnationally*, edited by Romana Huk, 375-83. Middletown, CT: Wesleyan University Press, 2003.

Perloff, Marjorie. "How Russian Is It?" *Parnassus: Poetry in Review* 18, no. 1 (1992): 186-209.

Perloff, Marjorie. *Radical Artifice: Writing Poetry in the Age of Media*. Chicago: University of Chicago Press, 1991.

Perloff, Marjorie. "'The Sweet Aftertaste of Artichokes. The Lobes of Autobiography': Lyn Hejinian's My Life." *Denver Quarterly: A Journal of Modern Culture* 25, no. 4 (1991): 116-28.

"Premiia Arkadiia Dragomoshchenko ostanavlivaet rabotu na neopredelennyi srok" [The Arkadii Dragomoshchenko Prize is indefinitely suspended]. April 18, 2022. https://atd-premia.ru/2022/04/18/statement2022

Samuels, Lisa. "Eight Justifications for Canonizing Lyn Hejinian's My Life." *Modern Language Studies* 27, no. 2 (1997): 103-19.

Sandler, Stephanie. "Arkadii Dragomoshchenko, Lyn Hejinian, and the Persistence of Romanticism." *Contemporary Literature* 46, no. 1 (2005): 18-45.

Shklovsky, Viktor. "Art as Technique." In *Russian Formalist Criticism: Four Essays*, translated by Lee T. Lemon and Marion J. Reis, 3-24. Lincoln: University of Nebraska Press, 1965.

Shklovsky, Viktor. "Iskusstvo, kak priem" [Art as device]. 1917. In *O teorii prozy*, 7-23. Moscow: Federatsiia, 1929.

Shklovsky, Viktor. *Theory of Prose*. Translated by Benjamin Sher. Elmwood Park, IL: Dalkey Archive, 1990.

Shoptaw, John. "Hejinian Meditations: Lives of The Cell." *Journal X: A Biannual Journal of Culture and Criticism* 1, no. 1 (1996): 57-83.

Silliman, Ron, ed. "The Task of the Collaborator: Watten's Leningrad." *Aerial* 8 (1995): 141-68.

Sloan, De Villo. "'Crude Mechanical Access' or 'Crude Personism': A Chronicle of One San Francisco Bay Area Poetry War." *Sagetrieb* 4 (1985): 241-54.

Steiner, Peter. *Russian Formalism: A Metapoetics*. Ithaca, NY: Cornell University Press, 1984.

Streidter, Jurij. *Literary Structure, Evolution and Literary Value: Russian Formalism and Czech Structuralism Reconsidered*. Cambridge, MA: Harvard University Press, 1989.

Todorov, Tzvetan. "Three Conceptions of Poetic Language." In *Russian Formalism: A Retrospective Glance*, edited by Robert Louis Jackson and Stephen Rudy, 130–47. New Haven, CT: Yale Center for International and Area Studies, 1985.

Tynianov, Iu. N. "O literaturnoi evoliutsii" [On literary evolution]. In *Poetika. Istoriia literatury. Kino*, 270–81. Moscow: Nauka, 1977.

Watten, Barrett. *The Constructivist Moment: From Material Text to Cultural Poetics*. Middletown, CT: Wesleyan University Press, 2003.

Watten, Barrett. *Total Syntax*. Carbondale: Southern Illinois University Press, 1985.

EU Authorised Representative:
Easy Access System Europe Mustamäe tee 50, 10621 Tallinn, Estonia
gpsr.requests@easproject.com

Printed and bound by CPI Group (UK) Ltd, Croydon, CR0 4YY